D0553340

Marking and Assessment

Also available in the Classmates series:

Marking and Assessment

Howard Tanner and Sonia Jones

:: continuum
LONDON • NEW YORK

Continuum
The Tower Building
11 York Road
London SE1 7NX
www.continuumbooks.com

15 East 26th Street
New York
NY 10010

British Library Cataloguing-in-Publication Data
A catalogue record for this book is available from the British Library.

ISBN 0-8264-6894-2

Typeset by Originator Publishing Services, Gt Yarmouth
Printed in Great Britain by Biddles Ltd, Guildford and King's Lynn

Contents

Contents

Series Introduction

Dear Teacher

Classmates is an exciting and innovative new series developed by Continuum, and is designed to help you improve your teaching and your career.

With your huge workload, both inside and outside of school, we understand that you have less time to read around your profession. These short, pithy guides have been designed with an accessible layout so that you do not have to wade through lots of dull, heavy text to find the information you need.

All of our authors have first-hand teaching experience and have written this essential series with busy teachers in mind. Our subjects range from taking school trips (*Tips for Trips*) and dealing with parents (Involving Parents) to coping with the large amounts of stress in your life (*Stress Busting*) and creating more personal time for yourself (*Every Minute Counts*).

If you have practical advice that you would like to share with your fellow teachers and think that you could write a book for this series, then we would be delighted to hear from you.

We do hope that you enjoy reading our *Classmates*. With very best wishes,

Continuum's Education Team

P.S. Watch out for our second batch of ten *Classmates*, to be launched in March 2004.

1

The Nature and Purposes of Assessment and Examination

What do you think of when the word assessment is mentioned? Perhaps you were always successful in school and university and think positively about assessment:

I was always good in examinations
I usually come near the top
I can show what I'm worth
I have a good examination technique
I'll be OK if I revise properly
My natural ability will take care of me

However, for many people the word carries negative associations:

I'm afraid of failing
I panic in tests and don't do as well as I should
Even if I revise I still do badly in examinations
I always come near the bottom of the class
Some people are just more intelligent than me
I'm just no good at mental arithmetic, drawing,
*   writing, PE etc.*

You should pause at this point and consider which of the statements apply to you and your own education. You should then reflect on the attitudes of some of the pupils you have known and how these might have impacted on their performance.

It is clear that some attitudes and beliefs support effective learning and teaching, whereas others stand in the way of progress. This book aims to convince you that assessment is central to the processes of learning and teaching and to help you to develop strategies to use in your classroom, which will encourage the positive beliefs and attitudes, which support effective learning and teaching.

Assessment means much more than examination, testing and marking. It goes far beyond the process of measuring pupils against standards.

Assessment is about information
Assessment is about communication
Assessment is about learning and teaching

Assessments can take a variety of forms and be used for a range of different purposes. We begin by considering the nature and purposes of assessment and examination.

Against what standard, by whom and for what purpose?

Prior to the nineteenth century, access in the UK to university and the professions had been largely determined by birth and patronage, but the changing needs of a developing industrial society demanded a larger skilled and educated workforce. The industrial revolution created an upward mobility, which was often mediated by education, and the professions began to develop formal qualifying examinations to control entry (e.g. Medicine: 1815; Law: 1835; Civil Service: 1855; Accountancy 1880). Such examinations *certified* the competence of members, helping to justify the status of the profession in society. To an extent they *broadened access* by admitting entrants from a wider range of social backgrounds. However, the intention was also *to restrict access* in terms of absolute numbers in order to maintain the status and financial reward of members of the professions.

In the 1850s Oxford, Cambridge, London and Durham universities introduced entry examinations. The main purpose of such examinations was *to select* those who were most likely to benefit from access to a very limited resource. An underlying assumption seemed to be that some people are more *intelligent* than others and have a greater potential for academic learning. Of course, success in entrance examinations was restricted to those who had received an appropriate education. During the nineteenth century this remained largely limited to pupils from the public schools (and the extent to which this still applies is debatable).

These entrance examinations exerted a backwash effect on the school curriculum with the knowledge and skills assessed in the examinations being accorded higher status than other, sometimes more practical, knowledge. The role of examination as a *driving force for the curriculum* continues to this day. Similarly, the distinction between high-status academic knowledge and lower-status practical knowledge and skills continues to pervade the system, in spite of initiatives which claim to establish parity of status and esteem.

During the twentieth century formal certification of achievement developed rapidly. The School Certificate (introduced in 1917) and the General Certificate of Education (GCE, 1951) both aimed to select out more able pupils who were capable of further study. The Certificate of Secondary Education (CSE) followed in the mid-1960s to serve the needs of the new comprehensive schools and to extend public examinations to the majority of pupils. It introduced a wider range of assessment techniques, and involved class teachers in the examination process. However, CSE courses and examinations quickly began to adopt the form of the more prestigious GCE 'O' level examinations. Instead of serving the vocational needs of the middle range of pupils, CSEs came to be regarded as inferior GCEs.

This dual examination system was replaced in 1986 by the General Certificate of Secondary Education (GCSE). Announced as being suitable for all pupils, it aimed to end the distinction between high and low-status examinations and to *motivate* middle and low ability pupils at a time of high unemployment. The GCSE involved a wide range of assessment techniques including coursework. The intention was to emphasize the student's ongoing learning rather than focusing solely on performance in the final examination.

The introduction of the GCSE served another major purpose – to provide political influence over the secondary school curriculum. Local examination boards, which were heavily influenced by the universities, had control of the GCE syllabus. Teachers had significant control over the CSE. Thus control over what was examined and therefore what was taught in schools, lay in the hands of teachers and educationalists rather than government. The GCSE, however, had to follow general and subject-specific criteria, which were determined by politicians (see Daugherty 1995). This central control was further extended by the introduction of the National Curriculum in 1988.

However, not only did government wish to control the curriculum through its assessment, it also wished to hold the system to account, to evaluate educational standards and *monitor progress* towards targets. The GCE and CSE were not suitable examinations to use as a basis for *monitoring and accountability* due to the standards against which they were referenced.

Norm, criterion and ipsative referencing

There are three main referencing systems used in assessment (see Wiliam 1992: 17–20). As a learner, you might think that the main referent should be whether you are improving against your prior performance. This is known as *ipsative referencing*. It makes no direct reference to other pupils or to criteria laid down by external authorities. This form of referencing has much to commend it, particularly with low attaining pupils who might lose self-esteem if continually compared with their higher attaining peers, or if they regularly fail to reach the standards set by some external agency. It focuses on improvement rather than failure.

Marking and Assessment

Some systems of assessment are designed to judge the performance of pupils against each other. This is known as *norm referencing*. Competitive entrance examinations (e.g. for the Civil Service) are norm-referenced, with the pass mark being determined by the performance of the cohort attempting the examination and the number of posts available. The purpose of such examinations is selection.

The GCE and CSE examinations were essentially norm-referenced, with the purpose of the GCE being to select the top 25 per cent in each subject. However, their norm-referencing characteristics ensured that they could not satisfy government aims for monitoring and accountability. If this year's cohort of pupils performed better or worse than pupils in previous years, the pass rate in the GCE examination would remain unchanged. As more young people stayed on in education and training post 16, the selective and competitive functions of norm-referenced examinations at 16+ began to appear less important than those associated with motivation, learning, monitoring and accountability.

Focusing on the quality of learning rather than competitive rankings leads to *criterion-referenced* assessment. Individual performance is compared with predetermined criteria based on the knowledge, skills and understanding required for the subject. The driving test is a good example of criterion-referenced assessment, as the success or failure of a candidate depends only on the knowledge and skills demonstrated in the test and not on the performance of other candidates. Candidates for the driving test know exactly what is required for success and are able to practise until their performance reaches the required standard. In criterion-referenced assessment, it should be possible to compare your current knowledge and skills with the standards required for success and to work to close the gap. Thus assessment can be associated directly with learning. When GCSE was introduced it was heralded as being a criterion-referenced examination which would motivate children by making it clear to them exactly what was required for success. Similarly, the National Curriculum incorporated *statements of attainment*, which formed the criteria against which its assessment was to be referenced. The definition of standards in terms of criteria has allowed successive governments to monitor the performance of the education system and to hold LEAs, schools and teachers accountable for the performance of their pupils.

There are a number of problems associated with criterion-referenced assessment and recording systems which we will discuss in a later section. However, the philosophy underpinning criterion-referencing is that you can work to improve your performance. This runs counter to the dominant theme of assessment and examination in the UK, which has traditionally been based on an implicit assumption that some children are naturally more able than others and should be selected out for privileged treatment.

Intelligence: a flawed concept?

What do you think determines how successful a child will be in school? If you pause to consider this for a moment, you are likely to come up with a list of factors, which influence the extent to which different pupils are able to respond positively to their experiences in school and learn effectively. Your list might include:

♦ The background knowledge which the child brings to school from home

♦ The match or mismatch between the home culture and that of the school

♦ Any disruptions which might have occurred to the child's education due to illness, moving etc

♦ Emotional factors

♦ Physical factors (which may or may not have been diagnosed) such as problems with vision or hearing

♦ Any specific learning difficulties which the child might have such as dyslexia

♦ The child's beliefs about themselves as a learner and the importance of education to their lives

♦ Their natural ability or intelligence

The last of these factors is the most contentious, but many schools seem to assume that children are born with a fixed, unchanging capability for learning, and plan the curriculum accordingly. Low attainment is expected from a large minority, which is simply considered unable to do better. This view runs counter to the attitude, held in many Pacific-rim cultures, that low attainment indicates that the pupil needs to work harder. 'Is a person's ability to learn changeable?' is a key question to be addressed before using assessment to plan teaching and learning.

'Ability to learn' is closely associated with the concept of intelligence. Some of the early theorists (Galton 1869, Spearman 1923) downplayed the influence of environmental factors and emphasized the importance of a general intelligence 'g' which they considered to be innate and unchangeable. An assessment of 'g' therefore, would allow you to predict the future performance of pupils. Shortly afterwards (1905) Binet published the first intelligence (IQ) test. Binet's aim was not to provide an experimental instrument to support Spearman's ideas about intelligence, which he criticized, but to identify those children who would need special support within the state school system (Gipps and Murphy 1994).

From the start, Binet was concerned that his test would be misused and that, instead of being used to identify those in need of support, it would be used to label children and set limits on their potential. Unfortunately, his fears proved to be well-founded (Gipps and Murphy 1994). Indeed, as recently as the 1970s, the eugenics movement were using Binet scales to test the 'feeble minded' and to enforce sterilization of women of low IQ (Lowe 1998). The controversy continues with Herrnstein and Murray (1994) seeking to use intelligence testing to demonstrate the 'biological inferiority' of certain races.

In the UK, IQ tests were used from 1938 in the eleven-plus (11+) examination to select those children, whose innate intelligence rendered them suitable candidates for an academic secondary education and reject those for whom this would be unsuitable. This was presented as supporting equality of opportunity, widening access and preventing wastage of natural talent.

However, for the majority of pupils, intelligence testing at 11 represented a barrier to equality and progression. 'Correct' responses in intelligence tests assume knowledge and values, which are dependent on culture and social class. IQ tests were originally standardized on whites only and they defined the nature of intelligence to suit their own cultural knowledge. From this point of view, intelligence testing is a means of social control aimed at perpetuating class inequalities and 'teaching the doomed majority that their failure was the result of their own inadequacy' (Broadfoot 1979: 44).

An alternative and more complex view of intelligence builds on the work of Piaget. He described intelligence as a form of adaptation through which people organize and construct knowledge as they interact with their physical and social environment. Intelligence is thus a developmental process rather than an innate and static quantity (Von Glasersfeld 1991).

This view is elaborated by Gardner who proposes a theory of multiple intelligences. He suggests that people have at least eight intelligences: linguistic, logical-mathematical, musical, spatial, bodily-kinesthetic, naturalist, interpersonal and intra-personal. We all possess these to varying degrees according to the interaction of heredity and experience, and apply them according to context (Gardner 1983, 1999). Consequently a much broader view must be taken of intellectual capabilities than that found in traditional intelligence tests (Plucker 1998).

The two traditions characterized above have very different aims and aspirations. The first believes that it is possible to measure an individual's innate and fixed potential to learn, in order to select the favoured minority for prestigious educational opportunity, thereby telling the others that they are just not clever enough to benefit. In the second tradition, intelligence is viewed as complex in character, not fixed, but developmental, and the aim of assessment is to devise individual educational programmes, which will exploit strengths, and develop abilities in areas of weakness.

These traditions are not only to be found in the world of intelligence testing. The beliefs about knowledge and learning, which underpin them, are to be found in much of the assessment which occurs in education. The purposes of such assessments need to be clear if they are to enhance teaching and learning.

The purposes of assessment

Assessment and examination data are used by a number of different audiences. You should pause at this point to consider the range of users of assessment information and what their distinctive objectives and requirements might be.

Assessment information is needed by a wide variety of audiences, including: the pupils themselves; you as their teacher; other teachers; parents; potential employers; other schools/colleges; governors; LEAs; and National Government. The distinctive purposes, which these audiences have, can be grouped together under three broad headings: *managerial, communicative* and *pedagogical. Managerial* aims for assessment include:

♦ demonstrating or testing the effectiveness of government policies

♦ holding schools and LEAs accountable for pupils' progress

♦ motivating teachers through payment by results schemes

♦ selecting pupils to benefit from a limited resource, e.g. university education

♦ controlling the curriculum by emphasizing particular forms of knowledge

Communicative aims for assessment include:

♦ providing information to parents about their children's progress against agreed standards

♦ providing information to other teachers, educational institutions or employers about individual pupils' knowledge and skills

♦ producing league tables of schools to inform parental choice

♦ informing teachers and pupils which parts of the curriculum are considered valuable enough to examine

Purposes of Assessment and Examination

Pedagogical aims for assessment include:

- evaluating the success of your own teaching
- analysing pupils' learning and identifying misconceptions
- supporting the teaching process by providing feedback to inform future planning
- giving pupils an appreciation of their achievements and encouraging success
- motivating pupils and holding them accountable
- supporting the learning process by identifying precisely what individual pupils need to do to improve
- encouraging pupils to develop skills of self-assessment and self-regulated learning

For more than a decade, educational policy in England and Wales has emphasized the managerial and communicative purposes of assessment at the expense of pedagogical purposes. When the National Curriculum was first introduced, it was claimed that its assessment would support five purposes, which were described as: formative, summative, evaluative, informative, and helpful for professional development (DES/WO 1988: para 6.2).

Although formative was listed first, the emphasis of the reforms was clearly on the summative aspects of assessment. The definitions of formative and summative provided in the initial guidance were quite limited and mechanical in nature. However, more recently, formative assessment has been characterized as 'assessment *for* learning'.

> *It is rooted in self-referencing; a pupil needs to know where s/he is and understand not only where s/he wants to be but also how to 'fill the gap'. This involves both the teacher and the pupil in a process of continual reflection and review about progress.* (QCA 2001a)

Summative assessment is 'assessment *of* learning' and includes both teacher assessments and National Tests. It usually occurs at the end of coherent units of work, at the end of a term, year or Key Stage. It is about making judgements about pupils' *performance* up to that point against National Standards and level descriptions. Such information is used for managerial purposes including communicating with parents and other stakeholders (QCA 2001a).

High-stakes summative assessment has been at the heart of government policy for more than a decade. During that time, the use of summative assessment over and above that required by the National Curriculum has grown rapidly (Harlen and Deakin Crick 2002). However, research evidence indicates that formative assessment is more likely to raise student achievement (Black and Wiliam 1998a and b). We will now consider the nature of the formal assessment and examination system in England and Wales and its impact on teaching and learning.

2

The Formal Assessment and Examination System

School children in England are now subjected to more external examinations than any other country in the world (James 2000: 351). They sit compulsory external examinations nearly every school year, with able children taking as many as 105 examinations. QCA are responsible for 30 million tests annually (Smithers 2002), at an estimated cost of approximately £150,000 000 (Carver 2000: 5).

The system is under significant strain. 50,000 markers are required for the written GCSE, AS and A2 examinations in 2003, but there are only 244,000 secondary school teachers in England (Smithers 2003). QCA is already forced to use graduates and students in order to cope. In summer 2002 confusion over the standards required for the AS and A2 examinations led to confidence in the examination system being seriously undermined. In such circumstances, doubts begin to arise about the credibility of the results.

In response, QCA intends to use computer marking and on-screen tests. The medium through which an assessment is conducted inevitably impacts on the style of the questions and the form which acceptable answers are allowed to take. For example, your understanding of a play might be assessed through

15

evaluation of your acting performance, through an open-ended essay about the motivations of a character or through a multiple-choice test which asks you to choose the date on which Julius Caesar was murdered. Clearly, the form of the assessment should be dictated by the knowledge and skills which are regarded as significant, rather than the other way around. However, all too often examinations and tests assess what is easy to measure, rather than what is important.

Reliability and validity

Any discussion of assessment must consider its reliability and validity. Reliability is essentially concerned with the extent to which assessment procedures give consistent results. Validity, on the other hand, is the accord between what is being measured and what someone thinks the assessment ought to be measuring. The distinction may be seen in the following example.

There is a small correlation between height and intelligence. If I wish to measure the intelligence of the pupils in my class I could measure their heights to a high degree of accuracy. This assessment would be very *reliable*, as other assessors measuring the intelligence of my pupils in this way would gain very similar results. However, the *validity* of the assessment is highly suspect, as it does not measure what it claims to measure. The high reliability of the technique and its ease of application might, however, make it very attractive to politicians trying to set clear and achievable standards.

Validity is a multi-faceted construct and may be judged in a number of different ways (see Wiliam 1992 for a review). The traditional form of validity is *face validity*: that is, does it look as if it will mean what it is supposed to mean? So, for example, our example of intelligence testing by height lacks face validity, as would assessment of a practical skill such as word-processing conducted through a written test away from a computer. An assessment has *content validity* to the extent that it assesses the content which it claims to assess. This is actually more difficult to achieve than it first appears, as few assessments deal solely with the content intended. For example, the Key Stage 3 mathematics examinations include questions in problem format. Performance may thus be affected by pupils' English comprehension skills in addition to their mathematical knowledge and skills. An assessment has *predictive validity* if it selects only those who will succeed. Of course, it is difficult to demonstrate that those who were not selected would not have succeeded if the opportunity had been granted to them. *Backwash validity* demands that we consider how the assessment results are used, and its social consequences – that is, the impact on teaching and learning.

Clearly, all assessments should be reliable and valid, but a tension often exists between these objectives which is difficult to resolve. For managerial purposes such as selection, high reliability is usually paramount. For formative purposes, associated with learning and teaching, high validity may be more important. Quality in assessment requires the provision of information of the highest validity and optimum reliability suited to a particular purpose and context (Harlen 1994).

Formal, external assessments underpin governmental strategies to raise standards. The managerial and communicative purposes of assessment have dominated over pedagogical validity, with significant adverse effects on teaching and learning.

In the original model for GCSE, coursework contributed substantially to the final grade. However, although teacher-assessed coursework has high validity in terms of learning, doubts were expressed about its reliability. Some politicians suspected that the high-stakes nature of the assessment might lead to cheating, and limits were placed on the percentage which coursework could contribute to the final result (Daugherty 1995).

However, even in external examinations, a significant proportion of pupils are incorrectly graded. In Key Stage 3 tests, about 30 per cent of pupils are placed in the wrong level (Wiliam 1996: 301, Black 1998a: 41). There is no evidence that external examinations results are any more reliable than externally moderated Teacher Assessments (Brooks 2002: 178).

The publication of league tables and target setting based on the proportion of pupils gaining key grades in external examinations has had profound social consequences in schools. The curriculum becomes distorted as schools focus on the subjects to be externally assessed. Teachers and pupils abandon the pursuit of genuine understanding, aiming instead at short-term memorization to improve test performance (Black and Wiliam 1998b).

In GCSE league tables the key figure is the percentage of pupils gaining five A* to C grades.

Pupils on the C/D grade boundary are therefore critical to a school's performance. Improving a pupil's grade from E to D, or from B to A, achieves nothing in league-table terms. Resources may be targeted at pupils who are on the C/D borderline in the hope of gaining more C grades. This inevitably disadvantages other groups (Gillborn and Youdell 2000: 133–65).

The GCSE examination also distorts the curriculum through differentiated levels of entry. Most subjects have two tiers of entry, a foundation level covering grades G to C and a higher tier covering grades D to A*. Although, in theory, decisions about the tier of entry may be left until Year 11, in practice a school's setting system often moves the decision point to the end of Year 9. This causes serious problems for student motivation. Issues of equality of opportunity also arise, with black and working-class students and boys being disproportionately placed in foundation tiers (Gilborn and Youdell 2000: 98–132).

Traditionally the Key Stage 4 and Key Stage 5 curricula have been treated as separate entities. Similarly, a divide has long existed between the practical, vocational and academic pathways, with academic qualifications being regarded more highly. However, 14–19 education is now being redesigned as a coherent structure.

Curriculum reform and the qualifications framework 14–19

The 14–19 education system has two central weaknesses: 'First, a weak vocational offer. Second, a narrow academic track – narrow in who was on it, and also narrow in what was studied. The result is a system marked by barriers to learning rather than support for learning' (Miliband 2003). The Dearing review (1996) recommended that the complex post-16 structure, with thousands of diverse A level, vocational and occupational qualifications, should be rationalized to a single, all-encompassing national framework (Brooks 2002). This reform aimed to encourage greater participation, and to create greater coherence, depth and breadth in the post-16 curriculum. It is also intended to develop parity of esteem between vocational and academic pathways through the creation of a flexible qualification structure with equivalence between the qualifications at each of six levels (Table 2.1).

All qualifications in the framework have to meet a set of common criteria, with additional criteria depending on the type of qualification (GNVQs, NVQs, GCSEs and A/AS). To promote flexibility in the curriculum and to facilitate the mixing and matching of vocational and academic courses, the structure is based on units of work of equivalent size and difficulty: a six-unit GNVQ equates to one A level, for example, and an Intermediate GNVQ to four GCSEs (grade A*-C).

The introduction of Foundation and Intermediate GNVQs to schools proved to be problematic, however. Few schools had sufficient curriculum time to include them in their Key Stage 4 provision; and they are now being replaced by 'vocational GCSEs'.

A new Advanced Subsidiary (AS) qualification was introduced by Curriculum 2000 to facilitate broadening of the post-16 academic curriculum. Designed as one-year courses worth three units, students might take AS

Table 2.1 The qualifications framework

Level of qualification	General		Vocationally related	Occupational
5	Higher-level qualifications BTEC Higher Nationals			Level 5 NVQ
4				Level 4 NVQ
3 Advanced level	A level	Free-standing mathematics units level 3	Vocational A level (Advanced GNVQ)	Level 3 NVQ
2 Intermediate level	GCSE grade A*-C	Free-standing mathematics units level 2	Intermediate GNVQ	Level 2 NVQ
1 Foundation level	GCSE grade D-G	Free-standing mathematics units level 1	Foundation GNVQ	Level 1 NVQ
Entry level	Entry level certificate			

(Source: http://www.qca.org.uk/nq/framework/)

levels in five subjects in Year 12, reducing to three in Year 13. AS levels were also intended to provide an intermediate step between GCSE and A level, providing better progression and thereby reducing the drop-out rate, but providing an exit qualification for those who did not continue to A level.

The new Advanced Subsidiary levels replaced the older Advanced Supplementary examinations, and the common title 'AS' probably contributed to the subsequent confusion over standards. The older Advanced Supplementary courses covered half the content of an A level, but at the same standard of difficulty. The new AS levels, however, were intended to act as the first half of an A level course and be examined at a level appropriate for that point in the course. Marks gained at the new AS level contribute to the final A level by being combined with the marks gained at A2 level.

Lloyd (1999) predicted that the new system would lead to a dilution of standards as awards based on different standards were aggregated to create a final grade. It was intended that grade boundaries would be adjusted to maintain standards, using statistical procedures. However, the late application of these procedures in a non-transparent manner led to furious public controversy over the 2002 results. The resulting inquiry (Tomlinson 2002) recommended that AS and A2 should be de-coupled to create two freestanding qualifications, and an independent review be held into whether standards were being maintained.

Maintaining standards?

Every year when examination results are published the debate about standards begins. If pass rates are up the government will claim standards have risen. However, the opposition and the press may claim that a higher pass rate is a sign of falling standards. On the other hand, if pass rates are down, everyone claims that standards have fallen! Teachers and pupils feel damned either way.

The confusion is partly due to differing interpretations of 'standards'. Do you set your standard through norm referencing, whereby only a set percentage 'pass' irrespective of how well students perform, or do you accredit everyone who achieves the criteria?

The A level is the oldest current qualification in the UK and is frequently referred to in the media as the 'gold standard'. This implies that it is based on criterion referencing where 'the achievement required for an A level should remain the same from year to year and reflect predetermined standards of attainment, irrespective of how many students achieve the necessary standards' (Tomlinson 2002: para 19). However, its main purpose has always been to select an elite group of students for higher education, and thus retains a degree of norm referencing. Offers of university places are usually conditional on the attainment of specific grades. If unexpectedly large numbers of students were to gain high grades, it would cause major problems for admissions tutors and result in a loss of trust in the 'currency' of the examination.

The marks gained in examinations are of little value in themselves – they depend on the relative difficulty of the questions set. The marks provide a rank order, but lack meaning. End users of assessments need to be able to interpret levels of performance. Setting a 'standard' involves attaching precise meanings to a particular set of examination scores (Wiliam 1996: 294). However, all examinations are unreliable to some degree. No matter how detailed and precise the mark scheme, markers have to make judgements and inconsistencies arise as different markers award different scores to the same piece of work. Candidates react to context and the precise wording of questions, performing differently on apparently equivalent questions. Examiners and teachers involved in assessment can develop a common interpretation of the standard to which they are working (Wiliam 1996) and judgements are made on that basis. This is known as construct-referenced assessment (Black 1998a: 74).

For managerial purposes, governments wish to monitor the performance of the education system, to evaluate the impact of their policies and prove to the electorate that they have raised standards. Teachers and students would like to be reassured that it is equally difficult to succeed in examinations set by different boards and in different subjects to ensure that the system is fair. Furthermore, they would like examinations to be predictable in standard, and to be sure that their achievements will be recognized by others.

Aims associated with selection may be satisfied by comparing students with others in the cohort and passing a fixed proportion, but political and managerial purposes require the ability to track performance over time. The political imperative for this is partly due to the belief held by each generation that current standards are not as demanding as they were in the old days. However, tracking standards over time is notoriously difficult.

The first National Curriculum SAT papers were designed with the intention that the average pupil in Year 6 and Year 9 should gain Level 4 and Level 5.5 respectively. So, can we just compare the standard required to achieve a particular level today with that demanded of the first cohort? Since its inception, the National Curriculum has been subject to almost continuous revision. The content being examined has changed significantly and the time devoted to core subjects has been amended. Similarly, the style and structure of GCSE and A levels have changed significantly, with modifications to coursework, modularization and the introduction of AS levels as an intermediate qualification. Such changes make a fair comparison difficult.

The problem is compounded by student choice and changing patterns of entry. The number of A level entries has almost doubled since 1988 (Weeden *et al.* 2002: 3). The cohort taking A level today has very different characteristics to the 1988 cohort. If we were considering the 1988 cohorts as norm groups, they would now be out of date. Similar variations are to be found in GCSE entries. If courses are to be followed by a much broader spectrum of the cohort, should we expect either the courses or the standards demanded of students to remain unchanged?

Many schools use commercially standardized tests to predict the future performance of pupils. These have often been referenced to the past performance of a large representative sample of students. However, standardization is an expensive process and usually only occurs every five to ten years, by which time the norm group may be becoming out of date and the conclusions drawn dubious. Many experts believe that the problems are so intractable that comparability of standards is essentially impossible to achieve (Wiliam 1996: 299).

However, the judgement of Ofsted is that standards are rising in English schools, with increases in the percentage of pupils gaining expected levels in SATs, five GCSE A* to C grades, and two or more A level or AS or GNVQ passes (Ofsted 2003). So are our children getting better? Well, scores on achievement tests usually tend to rise over time as teachers and students become more familiar with the requirements of the examinations and prepare better for them. There is, however, a fine line between this and teaching to the test. Examinations focus on forms of knowledge and skills which can be assessed in timed written papers, at the expense of higher-level thinking. Teaching to the test often leads to a narrowing of the curriculum, restricting learning to the practice of predictable test items.

The achievement of good examination results should not be the sole purpose of education. For example, in the Third International Mathematics and Science Study (TIMSS), Japan was one of the highest scoring countries in Science at age 13, but had one of the lowest proportions of students saying that they liked Science (Beaton *et al.* 1996). Our aim should be to produce young adults who understand their work well enough to be able to apply it in the world outside of the examination hall. They should also wish to be lifelong learners, enthused with the desire to follow their studies further. This should apply to all groups of learners. However, there is growing concern about the relative performance of boys and girls.

Gender issues in assessment

Twenty-five years ago girls' performance was the focus of concern, but more recently the issue has become the perceived under-performance of boys. Popular accounts attribute this to girls' hard work and boys' laddish subculture. Boys are perceived to be under-achieving due to their own innate failings and inappropriate behaviours (Salisbury *et al.* 1999, Gorard 2001: 4–8). This has led to numerous projects designed to remedy boys' underachievement through experiments with teaching style, single sex classes, etc. (Thornton 1999), and government targets and strategies aim to close the gap (DfEE 2003).

Unfortunately, there is little evidence to support this dominant account. Prior to the introduction of GCSE and the National Curriculum, girls were slightly ahead of boys in 16+ examinations by about 2 percentage points. However, 1987/88 and 1988/89 saw big increases in the girls' advantage over the boys. During this period norm referencing, which had maintained results at a fairly stable level, ended and the proportion of students gaining A to C grades increased rapidly. From 1990 onwards, the situation stabilized again, with overall results still showing an upward trend, but with the girl–boy performance gap remarkably stable at approximately 10 percentage points. Closer examination of the statistics reveals dramatic changes in the relative pass rates of boys and girls in certain key subjects. For example, the change from O level to

GCSE resulted in the girl–boy performance advantage increasing from 3.7 per cent to 13.7 per cent in English, −3.1 to 5.7 per cent in History and −0.1 per cent to 6.1 per cent in Geography (Stobart *et al.* 1992a: 273).

The rapidity of the change over a period of about two years, followed by a return to a stable but increased performance gap, seems to suggest that the prime cause is the nature of the examination process itself and the re-definition of subjects, which occurred during the introduction of GCSE and the National Curriculum (Gorard 2001: 9–12).

As the performance gap is stable and probably the result of the examination process itself rather than some underlying educational problem, Gorard (2001: 9–12) suggests that there should be no particular urgency in seeking to close it. However, this neglects the potential long-term impact on boys' self-esteem and their attitude to schooling. For it is not only in GCSE that a gender-based performance gap exists. The SAT examinations show a consistent advantage to the girls in all three core subjects at Key Stage 1. At Key Stage 2 the girls outperform the boys in English and Mathematics, with Science results being roughly equal. At Key Stage 3, Science and Mathematics results are very similar, but the girls' advantage in English remains consistently very strong at roughly 17 percentage points (DfEE 2003). The boys' persistent under-performance in English is particularly concerning, given its significance for the learning of other subjects, and because it is required for entry to higher-level courses.

Teacher assessments (TA) demonstrate a greater advantage to girls than examinations in most subjects

(Gorard *et al.* 1999). Possibly, given that some groups of boys demonstrate less commitment to school values, discipline and homework than girls (OHMCI 1997, Harris *et al.* 1993), TA may be reflecting effort and compliance. Causality is unclear, but a vicious circle may exist here for some low-attaining boys, with poor performance leading to reduced self-esteem and lack of commitment to school values, which in turn lowers performance.

International comparisons seem to indicate that large gender differences are not inevitable (OECD 2000). For example, the Mathematics results for 14 year-old pupils reported in the TIMSS study show an advantage to the boys in the same year that girls gained higher scores than boys in the KS3 SATs (Beaton *et al.* 1996). The form and character of the examination can make significant differences to the relative performance of boys and girls.

On average, multiple-choice examinations tend to favour boys, whereas girls do better on free response or essay-type answers (Gipps and Murphy 1994, DfEE 2003). This has sometimes been reported as multiple-choice questions favour boys due to their greater willingness to take chances and guess. However, an alternative interpretation might be that testing via essay response has limited validity, due to the interference of language skills in the assessment.

The context in which questions are placed affects success rates differentially in a stereotypical manner (Gipps and Murphy 1994, Boaler 1994, DfEE 2003). Context preference is becoming less stereotypical, but in one direction, with girls willing to operate in male contexts, but boys less able to work in traditionally female contexts. A similar effect exists in subject choice (DfEE 2003).

There is a perception that assessment based on coursework favours girls, whereas boys do better in terminal examinations (DfEE 2003) and that it was the introduction of coursework in GCSE, which led to the gender gap widening. However, coursework marks were in line with those from terminal examinations (Stobart *et al.* 1992a), although the analysis did not include coursework that was not handed in (more often boys than girls). Doing coursework should be a learning experience, not merely an assessment event, and it may be that students who work hard at their coursework do better in terminal examinations as a result. If, on average, girls put in more effort and thus gain better marks in both coursework and examination, surely this is only fair?

But what is fair and equitable in terms of assessment? The assessment system in England and Wales now seems to privilege girls at every level. Selection procedures based on such assessments may be consigning boys to lower-status sets or courses from which it is difficult to escape. You need to be aware of the potential bias of certain modes of assessment when making decisions based on examination and assessment data.

You also need to recognize the impact which continuous failure or poor performance in formal assessment can have on students' self-esteem and their engagement with school culture. The most important issue for teachers is how to use assessment, both formal and informal, to foster motivation, self-esteem and a desire for lifelong learning in all students.

3
Recording and Reporting

Planning for assessment

Assessment is central to the process of teaching and learning and forms an important element in the lives of pupils and teachers. During the school year, a significant amount of time and effort is spent on assessing, marking, testing, examining and reporting. This has a big impact on students, who react emotionally to the assessment regimes in which they find themselves. The way assessment is organized in a school, department or classroom plays a major role in creating the culture, attitudes and norms of behaviour which shape the learning process. However, it requires careful planning to ensure that the regime in your classroom fosters motivation, self-esteem and a desire for lifelong learning in all your students.

In recent years, increased emphasis has been placed on summative assessment and, although this is occasionally useful to you as a teacher, it most often supports managerial purposes. However, it is formative aspects of assessment that support your professional aims most directly and can make the biggest contribution to improving attainment. Undoubtedly your school and department will have an assessment policy, which should detail some of the basic conditions, which your assessment practices must fulfil. It may even describe some of the principles, which should underpin the processes. However, planning for effective assessment is probably the hardest part of the job for novices and even experienced teachers to learn to do well.

Teachers sometimes have negative feelings about assessment, often associating it with unnecessary bureaucracy, and guilt about jobs on which they have fallen behind. However, the assessment regime in your classroom ought to be closely associated with your beliefs about the nature of teaching and learning and with the aims you are hoping to achieve.

In order to be able to assess effectively, you need to be very clear about the aims of your teaching. All your teaching episodes should have clear learning outcomes – what you want to teach and what you need to assess are inseparable. These should lead you naturally to conclusions about what you would demand from students to demonstrate their attainment. For example, what do you consider necessary to demonstrate achievement of factual knowledge in your subject? Repetition of the fact immediately after teaching? Repetition after a couple of weeks? Repetition when jumbled up with lots of other facts? Using it in a slightly different context? Using it in a problem-solving context? Justifying or proving it?

You may find it helpful to break down your learning objectives into categories to ensure that you consider the full range of your subject. One popular general classification is SACK – skills, attitudes, concepts and knowledge. Outcomes for a single lesson need to be a subset of those describing the whole unit of work. It is unwise to have more than half a dozen learning objectives for a single lesson, and fewer still will be easier to manage.

It is not possible to assess everything that a pupil does. Just as you have to prepare your lessons, assessment also has to be planned for maximum effectiveness. At a very practical level, you have to decide *what* you will assess, *when* and *how*.

WYTIWYG – *What You Test Is What You Get*, may help you determine *what* should be assessed. Pupils judge what you value in their work by what you assess. Assessments, which test only memorization, undervalue creativity and imagination. If you value the ability to apply knowledge and skills to problems you should assess problem-solving. We must ensure that we assess what is important rather than that which is convenient.

When to assess? Unless reinforced through revision, learning, as indicated by test performance, usually appears to decay over time. An assessment made immediately after teaching will appear unreliable when compared with assessments made later on. It is important to understand that every assessment is a snapshot of a moving target and dates rapidly. Being able to reproduce a skill, or concept after a few days or weeks does not imply that it will be retained for a longer period. When deciding when or how to assess, it is helpful to consider short, medium and long-term assessment separately.

Short-term assessments should form an informal part of every lesson. Teaching is a highly complex activity and demands flexible planning, capable of adapting to feedback from individuals and classes as the lesson develops. Two common forms of short-term assessment contribute to flexible planning: informal baseline assessment to determine prior knowledge and misconceptions prior to teaching; and dynamic assessment of the amount of support required by individuals during teaching interactions. Ideally, most short-term assessments will be obsolete by the end of the lesson or unit of work as the pupils learn and progress.

It might seem that the optimum scenario for effective learning would be for pupils to be assessed prior to a topic and then to follow individual programmes designed to address their weaknesses. Such programmes would allow pupils to progress at their 'own pace'. Unfortunately, for some pupils their own pace is extremely slow or even a dead stop! Such programmes overlook the social nature of learning within schools. Pupils progress faster when teachers drive learning forwards, using their knowledge of individual pupils to set appropriate short-term targets, but dealing with the whole class as a social unit.

Medium-term assessments are used to monitor pupils' progress over a topic, half term or term. They are more summative in character but may be used formatively to help plan forthcoming work or to set targets for pupils. It may seem logical to test at the very end of a topic but this is not the most effective mode of continuous assessment. Formative advice given as a result of the assessment is received after pupils have finished working on that topic and have moved on to something new. If you assess just prior to completing the topic then pupils may be able to act on your comments to remedy weaknesses and improve their learning.

As well as their summative purposes, long-term assessments are managerial in character. Pupils' progress may be measured against national standards or the key objectives for a Key Stage, allowing managers of the system to hold teachers, schools or LEAs accountable, or to judge the impact of an initiative. These assessments may also provide useful information about standards for the next teachers of the pupils.

Schools usually undertake a summative assessment of their pupils at least once a year. These assessments are often based on the results of school tests or examinations, which summarize the work of the year or the term. These examinations are often very formal, time-consuming, disrupt the timetable and represent a significant event in pupils' school lives. However, their precise purpose is not always clear beyond providing an apparently objective item to include on a school report! They may also be used to justify allocating a pupil to a particular ability set or course. However, you might question whether the time and emotion invested in such examinations is worth the effort for such limited purposes. Surely good teachers should know their pupils well enough to discuss their progress with parents or to judge if they are misplaced in a class?

How you assess your students should depend on the purpose of the assessment. Summative assessments required for class or school transfer should concentrate on 'robust knowledge' and are probably best served by delayed assessment. When school examinations have high status, they can motivate some children to revise work, although few know how to do this effectively without significant intervention from teachers. There is also evidence that when the focus is on competition and comparisons between pupils, there is a negative impact on the development of some groups of pupils. While competition can be a powerful motivator, the losers in the competition often begin to believe that they lack natural ability, leading them to 'retire hurt', losing the motivation to learn (Black 1998b: 43).

Formative aims may be served by many different forms of assessment events, drawn from a wide variety of contexts, formal or informal, including for example, scrutiny and marking of written work done in class or at home, short tests, longer examinations, extended project work, or oral presentations. The issue is not so much the form of the assessment but the actions, which are taken after the assessment event, to improve learning. However, formative aims are often well served through immediate or dynamic assessment conducted informally during classroom interactions. Data arising from formative assessment is often transitory, becoming outdated as it is acted on during the lesson and thus not worth recording.

Indeed, the recording of any assessment is problematic. What pupils seemed to know last week may now be partly forgotten, or have been amended and enhanced as they continued learning. Given such difficulties, you might consider why we bother to record attainment.

Why do we record attainment?

Although there are some statutory requirements, such as at least one annual report to parents, record keeping remains an area where professional discretion rules. You are obliged to retain records which detail academic progress and attainment in addition to non-academic achievements. These records must be updated at least annually. There are two questions which schools, departments and teachers must address if their recording and reporting procedures are to be useful and coherent. Why are we recording this information? What form should the record take?

Any recording system must have a clear sense of purpose to avoid the collection of information for its own sake rather than for educational objectives. According to official sources, the main reasons for recording pupils' attainment are: to inform the planning of future work; to enable teachers to make judgements against National Curriculum and other external criteria; to help teachers and pupils be aware of progress; and to inform reporting to parents (SEAC 1991: 2). However, we believe that there are some priorities, which should be considered when devising recording systems.

Recording systems should support formative assessment, by providing teachers of new classes and pupils with baseline data, which are easy to interpret, to support continuity and progression. Records should support the monitoring of progress and target setting for individuals and for whole classes. They should support personal reflection by both pupils and teachers when reviewing achievement. However, most of all they should be manageable.

In the early days of the National Curriculum, enormous amounts of teacher time, effort and goodwill were squandered on the collection of vast quantities of attainment data and the creation of records, which could not be used for any sensible purpose (Tanner 1992). Complex recording systems were devised based on tick boxes: one line drawn in the box meant 'has met the topic'; two lines meant 'can use knowledge to solve problems' and a shaded box 'real understanding has been achieved'! Unfortunately, even pupils whose boxes had been shaded persisted in forgetting things! Such records are too unreliable to be useful. Sadly, more recent official guidance continues to recommend such systems. The Key Stage 3 National Strategy for Mathematics (DfEE 2001: 141), for example, suggests that pupils' progress against key objectives should be recorded on class record sheets, updated every six weeks. The date on which a pupil achieves a key objective should also be recorded. Why exactly this would be useful is not made clear.

Many record-keeping systems still suffer from an absence of educational purpose and the collection of marks to fill up records is often given a higher priority than the analysis of pupils' work to discern learning needs (Black and Wiliam 1998b: 6). Ofsted (1998: 93) reported that, although the recording of pupil progress was improving, the results were generally underused, which suggests that sadly, in many schools, recording remains an end in itself.

What assessment records should you keep?

When devising a recording system, it often helps to identify clearly the target audience. For example, records for your own personal use may be very idiosyncratic and take the form of notes, but records for other teachers, pupils or parents will have to be more formal. The level of detail required should depend on the purpose for which the record is being maintained. If too much detail is included, intelligibility and manageability are compromised, end users are unable to see the wood for the trees, and you are unlikely to be able to keep the record up to date.

When formal school records are required, the use of ICT should be considered. Such systems should completely replace paper-based recording systems rather than duplicate them. There is little point in copying grades from one record to another! Once data have been entered, they can be stored, manipulated and analysed for multiple purposes. It becomes easier to compare and contrast the performance of students in different contexts. Teachers as well as pastoral and curriculum managers are empowered to monitor and evaluate performance and to set targets for the future.

Of course, the old computer adage GIGO (Garbage In – Garbage Out) still applies whether the system is paper-based or computer-based. If records are to be kept, over and above the contents of pupils' exercise books and teachers' day-to-day mark books, we consider that they should be:

♦ valid, in that they assess children against appropriate learning objectives

♦ reliable, in that they can be trusted to indicate knowledge which is secure, and not forgotten shortly after the assessment

- useful for communication with parents about children's progress

- helpful when making judgements against National Curriculum and other external criteria

- useful for long-term planning

- manageable

(Tanner et al. 2002: 103)

Few existing record systems meet all of these criteria.

We would argue that you should avoid having to record any information twice. A detailed departmental scheme of work combined with the day-to-day notes in your teacher planner usually provide sufficient information about what has been taught to whole classes. You need then only note unexpected performances from individual pupils or any particular difficulties encountered. Such notes can contribute to the evaluation and enhancement of your teaching. As part of your lesson planning you should prepare your key questions and other assessment activities, and it may be helpful to leave space to annotate them with some of the more unusual or interesting responses they elicited. Such informal notes provide a useful reminder of transitory assessment data and are helpful for planning future teaching.

Pupils' exercise books and files form a record of their ongoing work. A selection of other aspects of their work, which may be required for formal, summative assessments, should be kept in a portfolio. This may contain coursework tasks, project work, tests, examination scripts, etc. Pupils should be involved in selecting examples of their best work and this selection should contribute to the target-setting process. Pupils' self-assessments and their agreed targets could also be included in their portfolios, although pupils should keep their own copies of their targets, perhaps in their school organizers. Pupils' portfolios provide an informative summary of attainment for discussion with parents and can provide useful evidence for moderating your assessments against external criteria at the end of a key stage.

You also need to ensure that the assessments you make meet the criteria listed above. First, your assessments must be valid. Tests and examination questions should be directly related to your key objectives at appropriate levels for the pupils. Including work from the levels above and below the target level for the class will facilitate differentiation and provide appropriate challenge. You should ensure that your questions address the objectives related to process skills and higher-level thinking as well as those associated with memorization of content. Where appropriate you should utilize genuine problem contexts and real-world applications. Remember, what you test is what you get, so if you want children to make links between your subject and the world outside school, and to be able to apply such knowledge, then you should assess this in your major examinations.

Second, if your assessments are to be reliable you need to allow sufficient time to elapse after teaching to ensure that pupils' performance is robust. We would suggest that you wait at least two weeks after teaching a topic before you make a summative assessment.

Marking and Assessment

Similarly, basing your tests on single topics may be useful for immediate, formative assessments for learning purposes, but will often produce unreliable data for records intended for medium and long-term planning. It also fails to assess whether pupils have made links between different topics and are able to apply knowledge in different contexts. We suggest that your periodic summative assessments include at least two or three new topics and that you periodically reassess significant key objectives from older work.

Finally, if your records are to be useful, you should analyse your assessment results to identify persistent misconceptions and areas where understanding is weak. Marks and grades provide no information for improving future teaching or helping pupils to set targets.

If pupils are to learn from the assessment then they need to analyse their performance, distinguishing between errors due to carelessness, poor revision and genuine misunderstanding of the topic.

All assessment events can be made to fulfil formative purposes, even if they were designed with summative aims in mind. All assessment provides feedback to students about their performance. Examinations should do more than provide a grade. They should provide an opportunity for students to review and reflect on their work, revising effectively beforehand and identifying areas of difficulty, which can form the basis of personal targets.

4

Formative Assessment

Research studies have demonstrated that high-quality formative assessment has a powerful impact on learning (Black and Wiliam 1998a and b). The size of the effect found in the studies was so large that if it were applied to all schools, the improvement in performance would be sufficient to lift England from forty-first to fifth place in the TIMSS international league tables (Beaton *et al.* 1996). For the average student, it would amount to an improvement of two grades at GCSE. Low attainers are reported to benefit even more, with an increase of three grades in comparison with one grade for higher attainers. Unfortunately, the research also shows that high-quality formative assessment is not very common (Black and Wiliam 1998b).

QCA emphasizes that effective formative assessment represents a key strategy for raising standards. They advise that formative assessment, or 'assessment *for* learning' must:

♦ be embedded in the teaching and learning process of which it is an essential part

♦ share learning goals with pupils

♦ help pupils to know and to recognize the standards to aim for

- provide feedback which leads pupils to identify what they should do next to improve

- have a commitment that every pupil can improve

- involve both teacher and pupils reviewing and reflecting on pupils' performance and progress

- involve pupils in self-assessment.

(QCA 2001a)

The terms 'formative' and 'summative' are not used consistently in the literature. These terms are often used to describe types of assessment, with some writers using the term formative to describe classroom assessment and summative to describe externally-imposed assessment or examination. However, we prefer to use the terms to describe the *functions* rather than the *types* of assessment (Brookhart 2001) and you should recognize that any assessment event, either classroom based or externally imposed, could be used to satisfy formative and/or summative ends. We take 'assessment event' to include: the preparation for the assessment by both the teacher and the student; the feedback from the assessment offered by the teacher; and the impact of the assessment on the subsequent learning behaviours of the student (see Brookhart 2001). The ultimate end user of assessment information should be the student, and to be considered formative, assessment should be used to improve student performance (Black and Wiliam 1998b).

However, formative assessment is also considered to have occurred when teachers teach differently in response to assessment data from their students, tuning their teaching more finely to their pupils' current level of understanding and the misconceptions they demonstrate.

How should assessment inform your teaching?

During teaching, formative assessment is essentially an ongoing and informal activity as you absorb and react to the way the class is responding. You can assess the pupils' understanding of the lesson in a variety of ways – by observing their facial expressions, looking at their written work, asking questions, listening to students' ideas, supporting discussion, observing activities and providing just enough support for students to progress. However, these only contribute to formative assessment to the extent that they facilitate feedback into the learning process. In response to such continuous informal assessments, you adapt your teaching, speeding up or slowing down the pace, introducing a new metaphor, making continuous judgements and decisions about how to proceed.

Such activities may serve a variety of purposes. Baseline assessment may be used at the start of a lesson or unit of work, to identify the range and extent of pupils' existing knowledge about the topic. Although you may know from previous records roughly the level at which the class ought to be, you should utilize the flexibility inherent in formative assessment to fine-tune your teaching to ensure that you are making appropriate judgements about background knowledge and are setting suitable challenges.

Marking and Assessment

Baseline assessment may also include the identification of common misconceptions which are held about the subject in question. As teaching progresses, formative assessment and fine-tuning continues though judicious use of questioning, observation, listening and discussion. Finally, at the end of the lesson, you should assess the extent to which they have achieved their objectives, with a view to planning their next lesson. A distinctive feature of lesson planning associated with formative assessment is its flexibility (Torrance and Prior 1998: 155). This is a far cry from the rigid, one size fits all model of teaching which might be encouraged by a naive or too literal interpretation of official guidance such as the literacy and numeracy strategies. This is a bespoke tailoring version of teaching!

However, formative assessment should not be a one-way process. During a lesson, students are continuously receiving information. When the information is roughly in line with their current knowledge they may *assimilate* it alongside their previously held concepts and ignore anything which does not fit. Alternatively, when the new ideas are sufficiently out of line with their current knowledge, they may need to develop new concepts to organize and explain the new idea. *Accommodating* ideas by building new concepts requires the active involvement of the student, who has to make a conscious effort, and is much harder work. Although some students will have a tendency to engage in such reflection naturally, most will only do so if encouraged and driven by a teacher. As they build new concepts students continuously check their version of events against the official version being presented by the teacher or other pupils, modifying and adapting it as necessary. In order to do this they need to have both time to think and feedback on their tentative ideas.

This interactive process is at the heart of formative assessment. Ideally, students should be given the opportunity to articulate their thoughts and have them confirmed or modified in a thoughtful, reflective discussion. Of course, it is usually impractical for every pupil to receive personal oral feedback during a lesson. However, many of the difficulties which arise will be common to several pupils, and when managing such exchanges good teachers try to ensure that sufficient pupils have had opportunities to express their ideas for the majority of opinions to be evaluated in the discussion. Teachers must also be careful to consider the 'silent' students in their classes with whom they have few direct interactions. You cannot assume a lack of ability, interest or motivation just because a pupil does not volunteer answers as willingly as the more vocal members of the group. During such exchanges, students are engaged in formative *self-assessment*. However, their teachers should also be using such interactions to assess exactly how much help they need to give for effective learning to occur.

Strategies for interactive formative assessment in the classroom

Feedback is a key aspect of formative assessment. Teachers gain feedback in a variety of ways and in return provide feedback for their students. For practical reasons, some feedback is delayed and occurs through the marking of work, which has been completed in class, at home or in tests and examinations. However, much feedback occurs in real time, in the cut and thrust of classroom interactions.

Research suggests that immediate oral feedback is more effective than written feedback (James 1998: 99; QCA 2001a). This is because feedback works best when it is given regularly and early enough to be still relevant. However, not all oral feedback is good. The quality of the dialogue is important (Wiliam 1999b). Students must be challenged to think and act for themselves. The best interaction between a teacher and a pupil offers the minimum support necessary for progress to continue. Similarly, praise is often regarded as an obviously good thing. However, although praise is a motivator, it is addictive and seems insincere when overused (Good and Grouws 1975; Brophy 1981). Formative assessment intends to modify behaviour and support learning, so oral interactions should be constructive but honest, and discuss how work could be improved rather than simply flatter.

The quality of feedback obtained through dialogue depends critically on the quality of questioning and the care with which responses are treated (Black 1998a: 114). 'Questioning is the most important factor in students' achievements of high standards, where questions were used to assess students' knowledge and challenge their thinking' (Ofsted 1996: 23). However, the dominant purpose which questioning serves in many classrooms is to direct attention and keep students alert and on task, by scattering large numbers of short questions around the class. As a means of social control this is very effective, but it makes only a limited contribution to formative assessment and effective learning (Wiliam 1999a: 17). The majority of questions asked require simple recall and fail to provide the kind of rich data required for formative assessment (Gipps *et al.* 1995; Ofsted, 1998).

Although closed questions are adequate for assessing lower-order skills and the recall of information, an over-reliance on this restricted form of questioning has negative consequences for learning. When the classroom culture is based solely on closed questions, students may concentrate on trying to gain teacher approval through the production of the desired response rather than developing understanding (Brooks 2002: 54). In extreme cases this leads to 'guess what's in my head' exchanges. Open questions, on the other hand, can encourage self-expression and extended responses. When students are encouraged to make extended responses, the classroom dialogue may be developed to a more sophisticated level, with teachers or other students asking follow-up questions and beginning to probe for deeper understanding (Wiliam 1999a).

In order for the question to be effective as a vehicle for formative assessment it must be sufficiently open to include a *problematic*, that is an 'unresolved or not trivially resolvable problem' which induces some purpose or tension to sustain a discussion (Ryan and Williams 2000). Problematics may often be developed from the common misconceptions which occur in all subjects. 'Rumours' is a useful device for creating discussions based on such misconceptions. For example:

Marking and Assessment

> *I heard a rumour yesterday that when you multiply two numbers together, the answer is always bigger than the numbers you started with. What do you think?*

Asking students to discuss statements such as this before presenting a reasoned case to the class can generate rich dialogue and open a window onto students' thinking, revealing misconceptions and encouraging extended discussion. However, in addition to the problematic, the discussion must be supported and developed through questioning by the teacher. This should be indirect in character, in order not to steal the problem by funnelling thinking. A sufficient gap must be left for pupils to fill using their own powers of reasoning. The teacher supports this through focusing questions and encouragement to engage in collective reflection. The resulting dialogue should be thoughtful, reflective and intended to explore understanding, giving all pupils the opportunity to think and to articulate their thoughts (Tanner 1997; Black and Wiliam 1998b). QCA offers the following examples of questions which can be effective in providing assessment opportunities:

- How can we be sure that ...?

- Is it ever/always true/false that ...?

- Why do _, _, _, all give the same answer?

- How do you ...?

- How would you explain ...?

- What does that tell us about ...?

- What is wrong with ...?

- Why is _ true?

(QCA 2001b: 12)

In addition to rich questions and problematics, students also need time to respond and reflect on their answers. Teachers do not always allow students much time to respond to oral questions. If an immediate answer is not forthcoming, help is given or the question is directed to another student. However, if the question is sufficiently rich to demand thought, then the 'wait time' between the students' answer and the teachers' evaluation should be extended to allow the student to reflect and expand on their answer. Wiliam (1999a: 18) claims that extending the 'wait time' to three seconds produces measurable increases in learning without causing lessons to lose pace.

It has long been recognized as good practice to begin lessons by explaining the intended learning outcomes, and to end lessons with a plenary session to evaluate the extent to which the objectives have been achieved. Plenary sessions provide an excellent opportunity for students to attempt to summarize the main points of the lesson for themselves. Engaging in collective reflection in a plenary can help students to formalize the knowledge which they have gained, and is associated with significant increases in learning (Tanner and Jones 2000a). Dialogues generated in plenaries provide opportunities for formative assessment, helping students to identify their strengths and to set personal targets for further learning. They are also excellent opportunities for the teacher to evaluate the extent to which teaching was successful and to begin to plan for the next lesson.

Monitoring and evaluating the success of your teaching – using value-added data

Evaluating the success of your teaching through formative assessment on a lesson-by-lesson basis is likely to have an immediate impact on your day-to-day teaching. However, it is also necessary to evaluate the impact of your teaching in the longer term and against accepted national standards. Increased requirements for accountability within teaching mean that you are likely to need to use performance data to demonstrate the quality of your teaching. Currently you must prove that your pupils are making good progress in order to cross the performance-related payment threshold. Your school and subject department will also wish to evaluate their effectiveness in comparison with national and local norms.

League tables based on raw assessment data are 'rarely worth the paper they are printed on' in relation to the insights they provide, as they say more about intake than school effectiveness (Murphy 1997: 33). However, research into school effectiveness indicates that individual schools do make a difference beyond the social determinants of gender, class and race (Mortimore *et al.* 1994: 316). Value-added analyses rather than raw assessments should be used to evaluate the differential effectiveness of schools and individual teachers (Mortimore *et al.* 1994; Nuttall 1990; Saunders 1999a and b). 'Value-added' refers to analyses of performance which focus on the progress made by pupils between their time of entry to a school or key stage and their time of leaving. Some analyses also control for factors such as socio-economic status.

Demands for increased accountability have led schools to adopt systematic statistical approaches to the monitoring of the performance of each child from entry to exit. The main aims of these techniques and processes tend to be managerial rather than pedagogical, but effective and fair monitoring and evaluation of performance can also serve genuine educational aims.

In secondary schools, the process begins with the collection of baseline data. At the end of Key Stage 2, the following data is available for each child: raw test scores; age-standardized scores by month of birth; levels for reading and writing in English, and teacher assessment levels for all subjects. Many primary schools and LEAs provide additional standardized data such as reading ages.

Despite this wealth of data, many secondary schools choose to conduct their own additional entry tests. Many schools purchase standardized tests such as NFER/Nelson's Cognitive Abilities Test (CAT). Another commonly used alternative is the family of tests produced by the University of Durham, including the Middle Years' Information System (MIDYIS), the Year Eleven Information System (YELLIS) and, for older students, the Advanced Level Information System (ALIS). These tests have been standardized against the past performance data of very large samples of pupils in England. Thus it is possible to make statements like 'Students with this score in the test on entry to the Key Stage were most likely to gain this score in the examinations on exit'. The items in the tests are chosen to correlate well with performance in the examinations at the ends of Key Stages. This is a pragmatic decision rather than one based on curriculum concerns. Thus the tests are high in predictive validity, but low in construct validity. Formative aims would be better served through the use of diagnostic tests linked more directly to standard curriculum areas.

However, value-added analyses like these are useful to schools in a number of ways:

♦ They allow schools to predict the examination results which might be expected from a particular year group. This provides data to explain variations in examination performance when schools are held to account.

♦ Similar predictions can be made about specific classes or groups of students, allowing teachers or subject departments to be held to account.

♦ It is possible to identify those students who are likely to perform close to significant thresholds, e.g. the C/D boundary at GCSE, facilitating the preferential targeting of key groups who might improve the school's position in the league tables. (We consider this to be a dubious practice, which is anti-educational in character – see Chapter 2.)

♦ Continuous monitoring of performance during a Key Stage can identify individual students who are falling behind their expected rate of progress, facilitating early intervention and investigation.

♦ They can form a basis for discussions about appropriate targets for schools, departments and individual classes.

Target setting for schools, departments and teachers

Utilizing statistical analysis of the performance of previous national cohorts against one performance indicator to set targets is problematic. First, the analysis is predicated on the belief that prior attainment is the best predictor of future performance. Underpinning this position is the inference that ability is fixed. Of course, in the large scale, there is a significant correlation between scores on such commercially produced tests and examination results. However, at the level of the individual the situation is more complex and other factors such as motivation may be far more significant. Second, the norms against which such tests are standardized go out of date rapidly. Given that pass rates are rising continuously, value-added analyses based on old norms are likely to underestimate performance. Third, a school may traditionally perform far better or worse than national norms. Up to 92 per cent of the variation in performance can be attributed to socio-economic factors in the school's intake (Gann 1999: 30). If your school is in a 'leafy suburb', targets based on national norms may seriously underestimate actual performance. Fourth, predicting performance on the basis of value-added analysis is far from being an exact science. The majority of schools achieve precisely the sort of results their intakes would predict and only the highest and lowest achieving schools may be distinguished statistically (Schagen 1998: 4). Furthermore, positions in league table rankings are unstable with significant variation from one year to the next (Mortimore *et al.* 1994). Fifth, most variation in performance is actually explained by differences between classes rather than schools. The suggestion is that it is teachers not schools that make the difference (Ayers *et al.* 1999: 1).

These limitations indicate that you should not employ data from such sources uncritically. A naive interpretation of value-added data can lead to teachers and schools having a distorted view of the potential of their students or a false view of their effectiveness. Such data should be used with caution, as one piece of evidence among many, when creating targets for schools, departments and classes. The professional judgement of experienced professionals who have detailed knowledge of the school and its students should always be used to place the statistical data in context when managers set targets for schools, departments and teachers.

Caution should also be exercised about the form of the target which is set. Targets, which are based on threshold performance (such as the number of students getting over the GCSE grade C threshold) are likely to lead to negative educational consequences. Threshold targets encourage schools and teachers to focus on the performance of one or two statistically significant students rather than raising the educational performance of the cohort. Targets based on the performance of the whole cohort are more likely to lead to a general increase in standards.

Target setting may appear to be a complex process, but in essence it is straightforward. What is required is a reasonable prediction of performance given current circumstances. To this should be added a challenge which is sufficiently ambitious, but potentially attainable:

$$Target = Prediction + Challenge$$

However, if the target is 'plucked from the air' it is unlikely to be an effective management tool. The target-setting chain from LEA, to school, to department, to teacher ought to involve a two-way flow of information in a professional discussion which considers statistical data, context and students at every stage. Furthermore, unless the discussion at teacher level involves a close analysis of the performance and needs of individual students, target setting will be reduced to little more than an exhortation to do better. The target-setting discussion has to agree appropriate targets for individual students and devise strategies to overcome any obstacles to individual progress, for example, deciding to instigate a reading recovery programme for certain students.

However, the process should not end there. In the end it is students who achieve targets, not teachers or schools, and in the next chapter we consider the effective involvement of pupils.

We end on a note of caution. We would advise strongly against providing parents or students with predictions of future, long-term performance. How would you have reacted if at age eleven a teacher had presented you with a prediction which indicated that, if you worked really hard and performed exceptionally well, you might have a small chance of achieving a grade D at GCSE, but that you were most likely to achieve grade F? Motivation and self-esteem may be far more reliable indicators of future success in school, and these are factors which you, as a teacher, may be able to influence. Furthermore, given the potential gains which can be achieved through effective formative assessment, we should not assume that performance is predetermined. Rather, we should be considering the forms of feedback we can offer to enhance, motivate and support students in their learning.

5

Feedback and Marking Strategies

Feedback is a key element of formative assessment. Teachers provide feedback to their students in a wide variety of ways. As we discussed in the last section, much feedback occurs in real-time two-way interactions as a part of the teaching process. However, feedback is also provided through the monitoring of pupils' written tasks, exercises, tests or examinations. Some oral feedback on written tasks may be provided during lessons, but for practical reasons the assessment of children's work often takes place outside the classroom and the feedback is provided in written form – marking. If marking is not planned effectively, the feedback can easily lose its formative qualities and be reduced to the summative checking of low-level facts.

If written feedback is to support formative purposes, certain key components should be present:

♦ a clear indication of the nature of a perfect answer

♦ information about the standard actually achieved

♦ advice about how the gap might be closed

♦ monitoring of the student's response to the advice in future work.

(adapted from Sadler 1989: 121;
Black and Wiliam 1998a: 48)

Marking and Assessment

Unfortunately, the everyday practice of assessment often fails to meet these criteria. According to Ofsted:

Marking is usually conscientious but often fails to offer guidance on how work can be improved. In a significant minority of cases, marking reinforces under-achievement and under-expectation by being too generous or unfocused. (Ofsted, 1996: 40)

Black and Wiliam (1998a, b) have identified a number of negative assessment practices which are often found in the UK. We suggest that you examine them and consider whether any apply to the practices in your own school:

♦ test questions encourage rote and superficial learning

♦ the giving of marks or grades is over-emphasized, while the giving of advice is under-emphasized

♦ an over-emphasis on competition rather than personal improvement teaches low-attaining students that they lack 'ability'

♦ feedback often serves social and managerial functions, at the expense of learning functions

♦ the collection of marks to fill up records is given greater priority than the analysis of pupils' work to discern learning needs.

(summarized from Black and Wiliam 1998: 17–18; 1998b)

Teacher assessment of students' written work tends to focus on low-level aims, such as recall. There is insufficient focus on higher-level thinking or critical reflection, and assessment records tend to emphasize quantity rather than quality of work. Similarly, teacher assessment of the National Curriculum has tended to be based around frequent summative tests, which imitate external examinations, with little or no feedback action (Black and Wiliam 1998a: 18–19).

The reality of classroom life is that teachers will be able to devote, on average, only one or two minutes per lesson to an individual pupil, so the marking of written work inevitably forms a major part of the feedback process. We must now consider how to ensure that the feedback from marking is formative.

Marking their work

Obviously, you will have to conform to school policy, but you should reflect on the forms which your written feedback to students might take, and consider how your practices might best serve the aims of formative assessment. One of your first tasks in a new school will be to determine:

♦ *What you should mark*

♦ *When you should mark*

♦ *How you should mark*

What should you mark? You might think that the answer to this is obvious. Surely you should mark everything? However, teachers who attempt to do this are misguided. To attempt to mark everything leads to what we refer to as 'flick and tick' marking in which the teacher turns the page, glances at how neat the work is and ticks. This contributes nothing to pupils' future learning and has the form but not the substance of assessment.

Not all work can be marked in detail; you have to decide which aspects should be marked by you. Marking which merely indicates whether an answer is right or wrong fails to guide the pupil's further study and so is a waste of a teacher's valuable time. Marking a limited number of indicative pieces of work thoroughly, with detailed formative comments, will contribute far more to the pupil's learning.

All work should be marked, but much routine work should be marked by the students themselves. This may be achieved by calling out answers yourself, asking for volunteer students to call out answers, or calling on individuals to explain their answers. This has the advantage that feedback is provided very quickly, while the students are still interested and the issues are still relevant. Furthermore, if students are called on to articulate their thoughts and explain their answers, the dialogues and discussions which result can turn into rich, interactive, formative assessment opportunities.

Marking done by you should be tightly focused. It should relate very closely to the learning objectives which you have identified with the lesson or unit of work. If you have been able to identify any common misconceptions which are usually associated with the topic, you may be able to devise questions or tasks to expose them. You should also prioritize in your marking the identification of the key features of the work that you intended to assess. These features should, of course, have been shared with the class in advance. You may, for example, determine not to correct every spelling or grammatical error, but to focus on the use of the apostrophe. You may also have agreed personal targets with students, and then prioritize these specific issues with individuals, perhaps by monitoring whether they have acted on the written advice you gave when you last marked.

When should you mark? For feedback to be most effective it should be given as soon as possible after the task is completed so that it forms an integral part of the teaching and learning process. Pupils' exercise books should be checked on a regular basis – your departmental policy will probably indicate the minimum frequency. We would suggest that you aim to mark on a weekly basis. Glancing quickly through self-marked work allows you to identify any important errors to be followed up, either as a class or individually.

Prompt marking can identify errors before they become ingrained through use. Marking an exercise in class is often more effective than returning the work, albeit with lengthy comments, after a long period of time has elapsed. If you have been monitoring progress on a task during the lesson you might be able to make some general formative comments which apply to several students.

If you intend your written feedback on a task or exercise to be formative, then the work needs to be returned to the class quickly. Ideally, marked work should be returned at the start of the next lesson. Students (and teachers) forget the detail of the work they have completed quite quickly and move on to new concerns. If the assessment is done during the teaching of the topic, there are often further opportunities for the pupils to implement the advice given in the feedback and for you to monitor that they have done so. This will help to reinforce their learning. Clearly, this needs careful planning in advance.

How should you mark? Teachers use a wide variety of approaches to marking work, including:

♦ an emphasis on mark schemes and grading, giving marks like 7/10, letter grades or NC levels

♦ emotional or ego support through the use of smiley faces, ink stamps saying 'Ms Jones has seen this work' or supportive comments such as 'Good work!'

♦ general comments related to the task such as 'You are too untidy'

♦ specific instructions or targets for improvement such as 'Show your working out' or 'Try to explain why she was so sad'

♦ correction of errors, e.g. in calculation, spelling or method, showing the correct version alongside

♦ an indication that a problem needs to be discussed, e.g. 'See me about this exercise during the lesson'

A significant amount of teacher time is invested in grading work. Often the grading process serves little purpose and may even have negative side effects. A mark or grade represents a summative judgement, which tells the pupil how well they did and nothing more. A mark out of ten tells you nothing about your errors or how you might improve.

Students receiving high marks are encouraged and show increased interest in their work. Pupils receiving low marks are discouraged and begin to lose interest (Butler 1988).

Research suggests that feedback based on grades or marks fails to change future performance (Butler 1987, 1988; Wiliam 1999b). In Butler's (1987) research, pupils whose feedback consisted of praise and grades increasingly attributed their performance to their ability, and performed no better on subsequent tasks than pupils who were given no feedback. However, pupils who received just comments on their work improved their performance in later lessons. Where pupils were given both grades and comments, the impact of the grade appeared to dominate and no benefit was found. Given the amount of time it takes to mark pupils' work, it can only be worthwhile if the effect of the feedback is to enhance learning.

A distinction should be made between *ego-involving* and *task-involving* feedback. Feedback should be task-involving, that is, it should focus firmly on the demands of the task in hand. Ego-involving feedback, focused on self-esteem or self-image, as with praise or grades, not only fails to improve performance, but sometimes leads to deteriorating performance (Wiliam 1999b: 10).

Feedback should always indicate what is wrong with the work and what needs to be done to improve. Advice needs to be precise, indicating the steps to be taken, e.g. 'Draw a bigger diagram and use a ruler'. Feedback to any pupil should be about the particular qualities of his or her work, with advice on what he or she can do to improve, and should avoid comparisons with other pupils (Black and Wiliam 1998b).

While competition can be a powerful motivator, particularly when it is between evenly matched teams or classes, it has strong, negative side effects when associated with the assessment of individual pupils. The losers in the competition often begin to believe that they lack natural ability, leading them to 'retire hurt', losing the motivation to learn. The danger is that they then try to build up their self-esteem in other, less appropriate ways (Black 1998b). This leads to the vicious circle we discussed earlier which links poor performance, reduced self-esteem and a lack of commitment to school.

Students need to learn how to ask for help and the ethos of the school should encourage them to do so (QCA 2001a). Feedback which invites the opening of a dialogue, like 'See me at the end of the lesson to discuss this' may encourage them in this. It is also important for children to realize that to get answers wrong is a natural part of the learning process. The most successful teachers emphasize that a wrong answer is an opportunity to learn, rather than a cause for teacher displeasure. To encourage this view it is important to dissociate criticism of an incorrect approach or misconception from criticism of the child.

Feedback should encourage students to reflect on their work in relation to the desired standards and offer them a mechanism to close the gap. Ideally, the gap should present a realistic challenge, which the student believes can be achieved through their own efforts and accepts as a short-term target. Target setting by teachers can sometimes motivate students by reducing what initially may appear an impossible challenge into a series of small, clearly specified and achievable steps. The intention is to convince students that they can improve their performance through their own efforts. In the longer term, the aim must be to teach them that they are in control of their own learning. To this end, students should be closely involved in setting their own targets and not be treated as passive recipients of teacher-set targets.

Target setting for pupils

Target setting is very much in vogue in the UK as the dominant mechanism through which the government are managing change in the public services. Target setting for students is at the bottom end of a very long chain of imposed and negotiated targets. However, a distinction should be made between *performance* targets and *process* targets. Performance targets are associated with the achievement of specified measurable outcomes. In education, performance targets are often expressed in relation to high-stakes summative assessment such as the percentage of pupils gaining Level 5 in the Key Stage 3 SATs. As we discussed earlier, such performance targets are transmitted down through the system to impinge eventually on teachers and classes. Process targets, on the other hand, relate to specific actions that are to be taken. In education they are often expressed as *learning* targets and tend to be more personal, often more short-term and are associated with knowledge and understanding.

Research into the impact of target setting for students on learning is ambiguous. When students have been actively involved in the target-setting process and challenging but achievable targets are coupled with regular progress reviews, Brooks (2002: 52) claims that they can be very effective. When the targets are very personal and clearly relate to individuals, children can be highly motivated by them (Clarke 1998: 96).

However, in many schools there is a large discrepancy between the rhetoric and the reality of teachers' and pupils' practices (Bullock and Wikeley 2001: 69). In many schools, the target-setting process is erratic, bureaucratic and time-consuming, with little or no evidence of any improvement in learning. Interviews with children reveal that the relationship between official targets and future actions is often hazy with most students having only a vague idea of their place in the process. Students report that targets are set, but that they are seldom monitored or their achievement recognized (Weeden *et al.* 2002: 50–1). When targets are not perceived as being owned by students and are not reviewed regularly, they quickly become meaningless and de-motivating (Bullock and Wikeley 2001: 69).

Often, the problem is that targets are set rather than negotiated and based on performance targets passed down from above. Most students would find a target such as 'Gain at least Level 5 in the English SAT' far too broad and long-term to engage with effectively and to adapt into shorter-term achievable sub-goals without significant teacher support. Performance targets are inappropriate for student purposes. Process targets which are focused on learning lead to higher motivation and achievement than performance targets (Black and Wiliam 1998a: 14). Performance targets tend to encourage students to focus on attaining the grade, rather than understanding the knowledge. They may also encourage students to focus on how they perform in comparison with other, higher-attaining students, and to make consequent assumptions about their ability, which they may regard as fixed and unchangeable (Brooks 2002: 52).

DfEE (1997: 10) claims that the key to effective target setting is to think SMART: targets should be Specific, Measurable, Achievable, Realistic and Time-related. However, like most acronyms, we think that it misses the point. We think that there are more important criteria which should be fulfilled:

- Targets should focus on learning rather than performance

- Targets should be personal

- Target setting should be seen as an aspect of formative assessment and planned to be an integral part of the teaching and learning process

- Targets should be monitored and reviewed often

- Targets should be achievable in the short term

- Students must want to achieve them

- Students should participate in setting, and have a sense of ownership of, the targets

In the end, formative assessment will only be effective if students act upon the feedback that they receive. Their attitudes and beliefs about the assessment process and themselves as learners are critical to their success.

Students' attitudes to assessment and learning

Unfortunately, school culture in England and Wales has over-emphasized the use of high-stakes summative assessment for managerial purposes over the last 15 years. When work is returned to students, they have two overriding concerns: What was my mark? Did I do better or worse than my friends? Most students make no attempt to use the results of assessment formatively. They regard their results as 'summary indicators of their success; they do not see them as serving their interests and do not look for feedback about how to improve the way that they work' (Black 1998a: 135). In fact, most students regard the regular summative assessments which they endure as being for the benefit of the school or their parents rather than for themselves, and as being intended to make them work harder rather than differently (Black 1998b: 43). This attitude is a major obstacle to progress.

A major element in the change which is required to take full advantage of the proven benefits of formative assessment, is associated with the way in which we encourage the development of positive beliefs about the nature of learning, motivation and self-esteem. When the attitudes of teachers and pupils tend to favour a belief that ability is fixed and unchangeable, students will be unable to take advantage of the positive messages which are contained in feedback.

Wiliam (1999b: 10) reports that when reviewing the impact of feedback, although most well-designed studies reported a positive effect on performance, 40 per cent reported a negative effect. In fact, the quality of feedback has a major impact on subsequent performance, which is largely dependent on the way that learners attribute their successes and failures. The extent to which students are able to take control of their own learning and use the information which is provided to them from formative assessment is conditional on their beliefs about the causes of success and failure.

Attributions of success or failure are usually determined by three factors. First, the extent to which you judge your performance to be determined by internal or external factors, for example, whether you attribute your mark to the quality of your work or to whether the teacher likes you or not. Second, whether your success or failure is due to stable or unstable factors, for example, did I get a good/bad examination result because I am good/bad at that subject or did I get a good/bad examination result because I worked hard/did no revision? Third, I'm good/bad at that, but that's the only thing I'm good/bad at, versus I'm good/bad at that, therefore I'm good/bad at everything (Wiliam 1999b: 10).

In the end, what matters is whether students and their teachers view ability as fixed or incremental. (You may recall the discussion about intelligence earlier and compare the issues.) Students (and teachers) who view ability as fixed will see every assessment event as an opportunity either to reaffirm their ability or to be shown up. Current high attainers tend to accept the challenge, whereas many other students (particularly boys) would prefer to be thought lazy and uncommitted rather than dumb and seek to bolster their self-respect through behaviours which are not encouraged by official school culture. On the other hand, those students (and teachers) who view ability as incremental are likely to consider ability to be trainable and to view challenges as opportunities to learn. For these students, formative assessment is likely to be seen as an opportunity to learn and improve rather than as a threatening situation in which self-esteem might be lost (Wiliam 1999b: 10).

For formative assessment to achieve its true potential in enhancing learning, our students must have attitudes and beliefs which encourage them to use feedback positively. Some students are already able to use assessment information positively to improve their performance in summative assessments (Brookhart 2001). This minority of more successful students has learned how to use assessment data to help them learn. They have taken control of their own learning and are able to assess their knowledge, identify gaps and set themselves targets for their learning. In the end, the main aim of formative assessment must be to enable students to take control of their own destinies and become life-long learners who are independent of the advice of their teachers: and it is to this that we now turn.

6

Self-assessment and Learning to Learn

Involving children in their own assessment

Much of the literature about formative assessment emphasizes the role of the teacher, because teachers are responsible for planning and administering assessment: but in fact, demands for improved performance should move our focus to the behaviours of the learners. Ideally, students should share the teacher's learning goals and plan to close any gaps between their current knowledge and the desired goal, monitor their own progress and evaluate the success of their learning. This is something that has to be done by the students themselves and cannot be done for them by their teacher. The ultimate goal of feedback should be to teach students how to regulate their own learning (Sadler 1998; Gipps 1994; Black and Wiliam 1998a).

If this is to be achieved, the feedback must enable students to:

♦ develop their understanding of themselves as learners

- be clear about what they understand and what they are unsure about – they must know what they know already. This is usually referred to as metacognitive knowledge

- know what they are trying to achieve – they should know their learning objectives

- choose a strategy to help them to close the gap – a form of metacognitive skill

(Sadler 1989; Black and Wiliam 1998a;
Tanner *et al.* 2002)

These forms of self-knowledge are metacognitive in character. Metacognition refers to your knowledge and beliefs about what you know and your skills for controlling your thinking (Flavell 1976: 232). Metacognition is closely associated with self-directed learning and concept development (Brown 1987; Tanner 1997). Engaging in formative self-assessment is likely to support the development of metacognitive skills, which are likely to help students to develop into more effective learners in other areas (Black 1998a: 133).

Research suggests that involving students in self-assessment can lead to very large learning gains (Tanner and Jones 1995, 1999 and 2000a; Black and Wiliam 1998a). Unfortunately, the LEARN project reports that fewer than 25 per cent of GCSE, A-level and GNVQ students had opportunities to assess their own work. Indeed, most of the self-assessment was very limited in scope, for example, using the answers at the back of a textbook or self-marking tests (CLIO 2000: 4). We would not class these limited forms as true self-assessment but as self-marking. Authentic self-assessment involves sharing assessment criteria with students and encouraging them to become actively self-monitoring and reflective (Brooks 2002: 69). Although some particularly mindful students might try to use self-marking sessions for monitoring and reflection, the majority of students probably do little more than tick or cross unthinkingly.

Early attempts to introduce an element of self-assessment into the SAT examinations were unsuccessful. The feedback was not positive; pupils did not know how to assess themselves. Most studies report that when students are introduced to self-assessment for the first time they find it difficult (Tanner and Jones 1994; Black 1998a: 128–35).

Many pupils lack a clear overview of their own learning and become confused because they do not understand the criteria against which they are being assessed (QCA 2001b: 5). They may then resort to guessing what would be acceptable to their teachers – defeating the object of the exercise. We found a similar problem in the Practical Applications of Mathematics (PAMP) Project (Tanner and Jones 1994, 1995 and 2000b). In order to assess themselves, students must first be aware of the nature of a good solution to the problem. They must have internalized the general characteristics of the assessment criteria for the subject to the extent that they are able to interpret them in the context of that particular task. In the early stages of the PAMP project, we found few pupils who were so aware. Furthermore, it was clear that self-assessment was a novel concept for many pupils – they needed to learn *how* to assess themselves (Tanner and Jones 1994).

Marking and Assessment

This is where peer assessment proves to be so valuable. We found that participation in peer assessment helped to teach pupils both about the nature of a good solution and about how the assessment criteria operated in the context of a particular task. It is only after they have learned to assess the work of someone else that students are able to reflect back and begin to assess their own work.

The criteria against which coursework and the process attainment targets (AT1s) are assessed tend to be expressed in general and sometimes abstract terms. Students require support to learn how such criteria are interpreted in the context of particular tasks. Showing anonymous examples of good-quality work produced by other students can be helpful and can be used to develop skills of peer and self-assessment (Jones 1992). However, students who consider ability to be fixed may regard examples of particularly good work as intimidating rather than inspirational.

The LEARN project reports the use of peer assessment of draft work in A-level English where the peer comments were then used to rework the essays (CLIO 2000: 4). It is in complex domains such as this that peer and self-assessment generate the biggest gains in learning, by helping students to understand the assessment criteria which apply.

Plenary sessions can be used to develop a shared understanding of the assessment criteria and the nature of a good solution to an open-ended task. During the PAMP project, pupils often presented draft reports to the class for peer assessment. Clear ground rules were established to ensure a safe, supportive environment for presenters. Students were encouraged to ask presenters for explanations of points which they did not understand: 'How can you be sure they are equal?', 'Why is _ true?', 'Will that always be true?' However, any criticism had to be accompanied by a justification and suggestions for improvement. The focus of the assessment was always on the qualities to be desired in the work rather than competition with peers. The most effective teachers developed a classroom ethos, which we described as 'a community of inquiry', which was mutually supportive rather than competitive.

Such reporting of draft work has a dual purpose. The overt purpose is to improve the final version through discussion and constructive criticism. However, the most effective teachers used plenaries to engage in collective reflection and develop the skills of peer and self-assessment (Tanner and Jones 1994, 1995, 2000a and b). In the early stages, teachers led the questioning of the presenters, focusing the attention of the class on the most significant aspects of an investigation. This was necessary because students did not know what sort of question to ask, or what aspects of a report might be significant. For example, to encourage collective reflection, teachers always asked: 'If you were to do this task again what would you do differently?' This focused attention on the processes involved in performing the task and the success or otherwise of the strategies employed.

Gradually, the pupils began to appreciate the form of discussion which was appropriate and to copy the teacher's style of question. More importantly, in time it became clear that students had internalized the sort of question which would be asked, were asking themselves such questions prior to their presentations, and were preparing their responses. When students begin to plan, monitor and evaluate their work in this way, authentic self-assessment is occurring and real gains are made in learning.

Students were sometimes encouraged to redraft their work after the plenary before submitting it for formal marking. The grades achieved following redrafting were usually higher than would have been achieved unaided, but this formative assessment forms part of the teaching and learning process, not a summative judgement for external examination (Tanner and Jones 1994).

Although the PAMP project was focused on the process Attainment Target 'Using and Applying Mathematics', many of the techniques are directly applicable to lessons that are focused on more straightforward subject content knowledge. In fact, in the second phase of the project we discovered that classes who had engaged in collective reflection through peer and self-assessment performed significantly better than their matched control groups in aspects of mathematics which had not been targeted by the project (sig < 0.1 per cent, effect size 0.2, Tanner and Jones 2000a). Their learning had not only been about 'Using and Applying Mathematics': they had learned to reflect on their learning and to assess themselves. They had learned how to learn and used their new skills when learning other material. A similar effect is reported by the Cognitive Acceleration in Science Education (CASE) project, with improved performance found in non-science subjects as children learned to learn (Adey and Shayer 1993).

Self-assessment can also be developed with more content-focused learning. Teachers who had been identified as particularly effective in the Raising Standards in Numeracy (RSN) project used reflective assessment activities in their plenaries (Tanner and Jones 2000b: 125–7). Strategies included asking pupils:

♦ to identify warnings which they would give to other pupils about to start the same task

♦ to mark the work of an imaginary pupil which contains standard errors and to explain why the errors were made

♦ to identify what is important for them to remember from today's lesson

(Tanner and Jones 2000b: 204)

Some of the most effective teachers in the RSN project regularly ended units of work by setting the class a competition to write a good examination question to assess the topic. The best questions were to be included in the end of year examination. Groups of students then presented their questions to the class, who attempted to answer them. The discussion, which followed, focused on why particular questions were 'good'. 'Good questions' were considered to be those which demanded knowledge which was seen as critical, addressed a common misconception about the topic, or were expressed in a slightly unusual form. This not only provided an opportunity for both teachers and pupils to assess the learning which had occurred, but also ensured that the class had a good set of summary notes for revision. More importantly, the pupils were forced to reflect on their own learning and the most common errors which they might make and the misconceptions which they might have.

Other useful strategies include appointing a pupil to act as a 'rapporteur' during the plenary to summarize the main points of the lesson and to answer any questions from other pupils (Wiliam 2000). Similarly, Wiliam describes teachers sharing lesson objectives with students at the start of a lesson. At the end of the lesson, students were then asked to indicate, perhaps by using tick boxes or smiley faces, the degree to which they felt that they had achieved each of the objectives (Wiliam 2000). This second strategy has the advantage of providing the teacher with a written record of the pupils' perceptions of their under-standing.

It is often helpful to ask children to assess the extent to which they feel they have properly understood the key concepts in a unit of work *independently* of their success in the official assessment tasks. QCA (2001b) reports a school using 'traffic light' self-assessment when reviewing half-term tests. The learning objec-tives associated with the unit of work were listed on students' record of attainment sheets. After tests had been marked and returned, students were asked to indicate the extent to which they felt they had under-stood the learning objectives associated with particular test questions. A green blob next to an objective meant 'I understood this and feel confident'. A green blob could be used next to an incorrect answer if the error was trivial. An amber blob indicates that they are 'not sure' about the topic, having some understanding, but lacking confidence. This might be used even if the question was correct in the test. A red blob means 'I don't understand at all'. Self-assessment using a system of traffic lights or smiley faces can help teachers to identify areas of the curriculum which need review. More importantly, it forces students to reflect on their own learning, developing their metacognitive knowledge and helping them to identify suitable targets for improvement (Wiliam 2000).

Written records of each student's self-assessment are again generated on their attainment sheets. These are cumulative and generate an ongoing progress report. The information is in a form which could be used to generate helpful formative discussion at a target-setting interview or a parents' evening. Such records are manageable, as the responsibility for maintaining them lies with students rather than teachers. One of the major benefits of self-assessment is that it tends to reduce the amount of time that teachers spend assessing and recording in comparison with the amount of time they spend thinking about, discussing and acting on the results of assessment.

You may be concerned that the reliability of self-assessment is suspect – that students might be over-confident or even cheat. However, we feel that this misses the point. Although reliability is at a premium in high-stakes, externally-imposed assessment events, in formative self-assessment it is validity rather than reliability which is required. The aim should be to improve learning rather than to grade students. However, it is worth emphasizing that most studies into self-assessment report that, when properly prepared, students have generally been found to be honest and accurate when assessing their own work and that of their peers (e.g. Freeman and Lewis 1998).

The aim of introducing self-assessment is to develop students' knowledge of their strengths and weaknesses and the learning objectives which they are being asked to achieve. Most importantly, formative self-assessment is intended to motivate students, to convince them that they are able to improve their performance in examinations and tests through their own efforts, and to empower them to take control of their own learning.

As we have indicated earlier, assessment and motivation are closely linked, with some students learning from quite an early age that they are losers in the educational race and that there is little point in trying. Sylva (1994) describes the early emergence of two types of learner: the mastery child and the helpless child. Mastery children:

♦ are motivated by the desire to learn

♦ will tackle hard tasks in flexible and reflective ways

♦ are confident of success, believing that they can do it if they try

♦ believe that you can improve your intelligence

♦ if they see another hard-working child, will say 'she must be interested'

In contrast, helpless children:

- are motivated by a desire to be seen to do well

- seem to accept that they will fail because they are just not clever enough

- believe that if something seems too hard there is nothing they can do about it

- tend therefore to avoid any challenge

- do not believe that they can improve their intelligence

(Sylva 1994, cited in Black 1998a: 133–4)

Students' learning behaviour is dependent on the interaction between a number of factors, including their interest in the subject, their desire to succeed at school, their self-esteem and their beliefs about themselves as learners, particularly their judgements about their potential to succeed. These factors are gathered together in the concept of self-efficacy (Bandura 1977). Children's self-efficacy is dependent on the quality of feedback they have received over the years and the extent to which the messages have led them to perceive themselves as successful learners.

Self-efficacy, metacognition and students' potential for self-regulated learning

Students' self-efficacy for a subject may be defined as their judgements about their potential to learn the subject successfully. Students with higher levels of self-efficacy set higher goals, apply more effort, persist longer in the face of difficulty and are more likely to use self-regulated learning strategies (Bandura 1977; Wolters and Rosenthal 2000).

Research also highlights the importance of metacognition if students are to regulate their own learning effectively. Metacognition includes three components:

a) the awareness that individuals have of their own knowledge, their strengths and weaknesses

b) their beliefs about themselves as learners and the nature of [the subject], and

c) their ability to regulate their own actions in the application of that knowledge

(Flavell 1976; Tanner and Jones 1994, 1995, 1999 and 2000a).

The development of autonomous, self-regulated, lifelong learners depends on the interaction of three linked psychological domains of functioning: the affective, the cognitive and the conative (Bandura 1977).

The *affective* domain includes: students' beliefs about themselves and their capacity to learn; their self-esteem and their perceived status as learners; their beliefs about the nature of understanding; and their potential to succeed in the subject.

The *cognitive* domain includes: the students' awareness of their own knowledge of the subject: their strengths and weaknesses; the general principles they are able to articulate; and their development of links between aspects of the subject (Tanner and Jones 2000a).

The *conative* domain links the affective and cognitive domains to pro-active (as opposed to re-active or habitual) behaviour. It includes students' dispositions to strive to learn and the strategies that they employ in support of their learning. It includes their inclination to plan, monitor and evaluate their work and their inclination to mindfulness and reflection. In particular, it includes the strategies which they are inclined to use when reviewing or revising their work (Snow 1996).

Proponents of regular, summative assessments claim that they motivate students to learn. However, this is not true for all students. In fact, a recent review suggested that target setting based on summative assessment often results in students (and teachers) emphasizing extrinsic motivation at the expense of intrinsic, and a focus on test performance rather than understanding. This often leads to shallow rather than deep learning, and damaged self-esteem for failing students, thereby resulting in a reduction in self-efficacy and effort for a significant proportion of students (Harlen and Deakin Crick 2002).

The political pressures on schools to use intermittent summative assessments of students' learning are unlikely to be reduced in the near future. As we indicated above, several negative impacts on learning may result from on over-emphasis on summative assessment. However, some of the most successful students have learned to overcome these negative aspects and are able to use intermittent summative assessment formatively to support their own self-regulated learning. They review work and engage in self assessment as a regular ongoing process and use feedback information in both formative and summative ways simultaneously (Brookhart 2001). The following conditions are necessary for this to occur.

First, the students' self-efficacy must be high. They must believe that their ability is not fixed. They must attribute their success or failure to controllable factors such as effort or revision, rather than uncontrollable factors such as bad luck or lack of ability (Bandura 1977; Black 1998b; Wolters and Rosenthal 2000).

Second, they must have metacognitive knowledge of their own abilities. For example, they must be aware of their strengths and weaknesses, how their knowledge compares with the potential demands of the assessment, what they understand and do not understand and the errors they are most likely to make (Tanner and Jones 2000a).

Third, they must be aware of, and be inclined to use, effective strategies for reviewing and revising their work and analysing their successes and failures. For example, they need to have strategies for planning and engaging in revision, identifying key features of their work and anticipating potential difficulties in questions in advance of assessment. After assessment they require strategies for analysing and evaluating their performance. And finally, they must be inclined to implement these strategies in the belief that their performance will improve (Gipps 1994; Tanner and Jones, 1994; Brookhart 2001).

Unfortunately, a recent questionnaire study of over 300 students learning mathematics in Key Stage 3 revealed that only a minority scored well in all three areas. Although most students had positive beliefs about themselves as learners, which would support future self-regulated lifelong learning, a substantial minority held beliefs which would be likely to have a negative impact on future learning. For example, 28 per cent believed that 'Some people just can't do maths' (Tanner and Jones 2003b).

Success was generally attributed to hard work, but a fifth of students blamed their failure on uncontrollable factors such as 'Being unlucky with the questions'. Students who attribute their success or failure in mathematics to uncontrollable factors are unlikely to apply effective learning strategies. However, even though the majority of students expressed positive beliefs and attitudes towards revision, other factors suggest that they are unlikely to apply their efforts to best effect (Tanner and Jones, 2003b).

The majority of students failed to claim appropriate metacognitive knowledge and this is of concern, as it suggests that their revision is likely to be inefficient. Students need a detailed knowledge of their strengths and weaknesses to regulate their learning effectively. Most students appeared to believe in the value of hard work and revision, but either did not know, or were not inclined to apply, effective revision strategies. The most commonly used strategies were passive or reactive in character rather than pro-active. 'Reading through their books' was the most popular strategy, and was the only strategy used by many students. This does not require active processing and is unlikely to impact significantly on their learning. Similarly, although most students realize that they should learn from their assessments, the majority 'only look at their mark' when tests and examinations are returned (Tanner and Jones 2003b).

Self-efficacy, metacognition and the use of self-regulated learning strategies are closely associated (Tanner and Jones 2003b). Causality is probably complex, but students who believe that their mathematical ability is not fixed and that their performance is due to controllable factors are more likely to employ learning strategies than those who attribute success or failure to luck or lack of ability. The more effective learning strategies such as 'working out what I don't know' and 'highlighting the important parts of my work' contribute to the development of metacognitive knowledge. Students with good metacognitive knowledge are likely to revise more effectively. Successful application of effective learning strategies is likely to encourage the development of self-efficacy. The resulting virtuous circle may become self-perpetuating (Tanner and Jones 2003b).

Unfortunately, for many students a vicious circle may develop, with lack of self-efficacy leading to a failure to apply effective learning strategies or develop metacognitive knowledge. Repeated failure in assessments may then reinforce 'a shared belief between them and their teacher that they are just not clever enough' (Black 1998). Breaking into this vicious circle is difficult, but we would suggest that attempts be made to teach all students the self-regulated learning strategies which are currently only known by the successful minority of mindful and metacognitively-skilled students (Tanner and Jones 2003b).

Teaching students to learn from summative assessment

In 2002/3 the Developing Effective Revision Strategies (DERS) project was funded by the General Teaching Council for Wales (GTCW). Two professional networks of teacher researchers were developed, working in Key Stage 3 and Key Stage 4, with the aim of investigating ways of encouraging students to analyse their own strengths and weaknesses and to develop positive beliefs about their ability to improve their own learning performance. Strategies which had been reported to be successful in previous projects were developed further in the context of the teacher researchers' own schools, and new strategies were devised and investigated (Tanner and Jones 2003b).

It should be emphasized that the project was not aimed at teaching children how to cram for examinations. The students involved in the project were mainly in Year 9 and Year 11, so high-stakes external examinations were clearly a priority for both students and teachers. However, the aim was to develop attitudes, knowledge, skills and strategies which would support lifelong learning rather than just improve performance in an examination.

The majority of students claimed to be willing to revise for school tests and examinations, but relied mainly on reading through their books. We wanted to ensure that students were processing material, assessing their current understanding of topics and comparing it with the demands for mathematical knowledge and processes made by the examples and tasks in their books. Project teachers explored several different ways of achieving this.

The project demanded that students behave differently, taking active responsibility for their own learning and applying significant effort to review and reflection prior to end of unit tests and school examinations. Change of this order is unlikely to be sustained unless students believe in the initiative and quickly see hard evidence of success in their own terms (Fullan 1991). To this end, teachers began the project with a serious effort to convince their students of the value of revision and preparation for tests and examinations.

Most started with what they referred to as their 'David Beckham' lesson, in which they tried to convince students that ability and success are not innate, but built on hard work and training. Skill in taking corners is based on practising taking corners, not a corner-kicking gene!

The first strategy, which all the teachers employed with their classes, was the creation of a separate revision notebook. These books were chosen to appear different from standard exercise books and unusual rules applied to them. Students were encouraged to express their ownership of the books by decorating and organizing them as they saw fit. Teachers set revision homework prior to unit tests and demanded that students wrote a specified number of pages of revision notes. The amount demanded varied according to the age and ability of the class, but was typically ten pages. A policy of zero tolerance operated, with doubling up if work was not completed to length and on time. Students soon learned how to spread work out, drawing large diagrams and showing all their working (usually a difficult thing to achieve!).

The books included examples copied from normal exercise books and examples made up by the student. A balance was demanded between worked examples and notes. Use of colour was demanded, with annotations coloured differently to notes and examples. All work was annotated with 'Beware' messages, indicating places where a mistake was considered likely to occur, and comments were added explaining why particular steps had been taken. For example, typical comments included:

- 'Be careful to cancel down here'

- 'Put all the Xs on the side which makes the total positive'

- 'Try to find a number they both divide into'

Comments such as these were often discussed during plenary sessions to develop metacognitive awareness. An emphasis was placed on using plenary sessions for collective reflection. Peer and self-assessment were regular features of plenary sessions, and all the strategies which we described above were used on a regular basis.

Plenary sessions often included students summarizing key points in lessons and writing their own notes and comments. Students quickly got into the habit of annotating work and normal exercise books soon began to include annotations, warnings and explanations. Students' warning tips and hints soon became a regular feature of many plenary sessions. Some teachers formalized this by asking students to work in groups to create 'end of module tips' posters for classroom display.

It's good to do notes as well because when you look back and think, 'How did I do that?' the notes remind you.

SJ, Year 11

Marking and Assessment

As students' metacognitive knowledge improved they became more adept at writing their own examples rather than copying examples from their exercise books. Some teachers turned the invention of examples into an end of lesson game in which one side of the class challenged the other to answer the questions they had set.

Some students even wrote whole trial examination papers for themselves. One girl produced her trial examination paper on her computer and included the full official rubric in Welsh and English alongside the examination board logo, which she had scanned in! Her school internal examination result was excellent. Other students attributed her success to her revision effort and more students became motivated to try the same.

Some teachers, recognizing the need for students to see the value of revision from an early stage, deliberately made the first unit assessment after the project had started easier than usual so that everyone could see improved performance and attribute it to new ways of revising!

> I'd recommend this revision to all pupils in any school. It has helped me a lot and boosted my grades. If I [hadn't been] told to do it and it wasn't made compulsory, I wouldn't have done it.
>
> SJ, Year 11

After examinations and module tests had occurred, major effort was invested in returning scripts to students for analysis, reflection and target setting. The 'traffic lights' approach was used successfully by several teachers.

Three main themes featured in approaches used. The first demanded that students articulate their thinking about their work and make realistic assessments of their strengths and weaknesses, identifying areas of potential difficulty. The second theme was to encourage students to internalize assessment criteria so that they came to understand the nature of a good solution and were able to assess their current performance against the ideal. The third theme focused on the strategies which they could employ to review work, practice examples and revise for examinations. Underpinning all of these themes, however, was the regularly articulated belief that all students could succeed through their own efforts and that ability was not fixed but was trainable:

> Some people find maths harder than others but that doesn't mean they can't do it. They have to put more effort into it so they can learn more things.
>
> MCS, Year 9

The project was short-lived (four months in total) but, even within that short timescale, changes in attitude and behaviour began to appear in most classes. Comments from students about their revision books reveal that they were convinced about their value and intended to continue using them:

> To help a friend with low marks to revise I'd tell them to make notes like these. When you look back at your revision book you know the key points because you've underlined them, and I'd say to write them out, and look at the example to see

what the teacher means, and then you can get a better understanding.

AV, Year 10

However, the project is attempting to cause a major change in attitude and behaviour and we did not anticipate overnight success. Our anecdotal experiences with a school that began working in these ways some years ago indicate that it may take as long as two years to teach the majority of students the kind of effective learning behaviours which we have described above. However, the improvement in examination results which accompanied the change seem to indicate that it is worth the effort!

The current obsession with reliable high-stakes summative assessment in England and Wales is expensive and unlikely to achieve the desired goals. We hope that in this short book we have convinced you of the importance of formative assessment for learning. We hope that in future you will aim to use all assessment events formatively, focusing on validity rather than reliability in the assessments you make in school.

In the end, assessment is only valuable if it changes the way teachers teach and students learn. The most important end user of assessment information is not the government but the student. If our students are to develop into effective lifelong learners, they must come to believe in their ability to change and learn the habits of formative self-assessment.

Bibliography

Adey, P. and Shayer, M. (1993) 'An exploration of long-term far-transfer effects following an extended intervention in the high school science curriculum', *Cognition and Instruction* 11(1): 1–29.

Ayers, P., Dinham, S. and Sawyer, W. (1999) *Successful Teaching in the NSW Higher School Certificate* (Sydney: NSW Department of Education and Training).

Bandura, A. (1977) 'Self efficacy: towards a unifying theory of behavioural change', *Psychological Review* 84: 191–215.

Beaton, A., Mullis, I., Martin, M., Gonzales, E., Kelly, D. and Smith, T. (1996) *Mathematics Achievement in the Middle School Years: IEA's Third International Mathematics and Science Study* (Chestnut Hill, MA: Boston College).

Black, P.J. (1998a) *Testing: Friend or Foe? Theory and Practice of Assessment and Testing* (London: Falmer).

Black, P.J. (1998b) 'Formative assessment: raising standards inside the classroom', *School Science Review* 80(291): 39–46.

Black, P.J. and Wiliam, D. (1998a) 'Assessment and classroom learning', *Assessment in Education: Principles Policy and Practice* 5(1): 7–73.

Bibliography

Black, P. J. and Wiliam, D. (1998b) *Inside the Black Box: Raising Standards through Classroom Assessment* (London: King's College).

Boaler, J. (1994) 'When do girls prefer football to fashion? An analysis of female underachievement in relation to "realistic" mathematic contexts', *British Educational Research Journal* 20(5): 551–64.

Broadfoot, P. (1979) *Assessment, Schools and Society* (London, Methuen).

Brookhart, S. M. (2001) 'Successful students' formative and summative uses of assessment information', *Assessment in Education* 8(2): 153–69.

Brooks, V. (2002) *Assessment in Secondary Schools: The New Teacher's Guide to Monitoring, Assessment, Recording, Reporting and Accountability* (Buckingham: Open University Press).

Brophy, J. (1981) 'Teacher praise: a functional analysis', *Review of Educational Research* 51(1): 5–32.

Brown, A. L. (1987) 'Metacognition, executive control, self regulation and other more mysterious mechanisms', in F. E. Weinert and R. H. Kluwe (eds), *Metacognition, Motivation and Understanding* (Hillsdale, NJ: Lawrence Erlbaum), pp. 65–116.

Bullock, K. and Wikeley, F. (2001) 'Personal learning planning: strategies for pupil learning', *Forum* 43(2), 67–9.

Butler R. (1987) 'Task-involving and ego-involving properties of evaluation: effects of different feedback conditions on motivational perceptions, interest and performance', *British Journal of Educational Psychology* 79(4): 474–82.

Butler R., (1988) 'Enhancing and undermining intrinsic motivation: the effects of task-involving and ego-involving evaluation on interest and performance', *British Journal of Educational Psychology* 58: 1–14.

Carver, G. (2000) *Tested to Destruction? A Survey of Examination Stress in Teenagers*, at *www.pat. org.uk* (accessed 1 June 2003).

Clarke, S. (1998) *Targeting Assessment in the Primary Classroom* (London: Hodder & Stoughton).

CLIO (2000) *'Could try harder' – The LEARN Project: Guidance for Schools on Assessment for Learning* (Bristol: CLIO Centre for Assessment Studies).

Daugherty, R. (1995) *National Curriculum Assessment: A Review of Policy 1987–1994* (London: The Falmer Press).

DES/WO (Department of Education and Science/ Welsh Office) (1988) *National Curriculum Task Group on Assessment and Testing: A Report* (London: DES/WO).

DfEE (Department for Education and Employment) (1997) *From Targets to Action* (London: DfEE).

DfEE (2001) *Key Stage 3 National Strategy: Framework for Teaching Mathematics: Years 7, 8 and 9* (London: DfEE).

DfEE (2003) The gender and achievement website, at *http://www.standards.dfee.gov.uk/genderandachie vement/* (accessed 1 June 2003).

Flavell, J. H. (1976) 'Metacognitive aspects of problem solving', in L. B. Resnick (ed.), *The Nature of Intelligence* (Hillsdale, NJ: Lawrence Erlbaum Associates), pp. 231–5.

Freeman, R. and Lewis, R. (1998) *Planning and Implementing Assessment* (London: Kogan Page).

Fullan, M. (1991) *The New Meaning of Educational Change* (London: Cassell).

Bibliography

Galton, F. (1869) *Hereditary Genius* (London: Macmillan).

Gann, N. (1999) *Targets for Tomorrow's Schools: A Guide to Whole School Target Setting for Governors and Headteachers* (London: Falmer).

Gardner, H. (1983) *Frames of Mind: The Theory of Multiple Intelligence* (New York: Basic Books).

Gardner, H., (1999) Who owns intelligence?, at *http://www.theatlantic.com/issues/99feb/intel.htm* (accessed 1 June 2003).

Gillborn, D. and Youdell, D. (2000) *Rationing Education* (Buckingham: Open University Press).

Gipps, C. (1994) *Beyond Testing: Towards a Theory of Educational Assessment* (London: Falmer).

Gipps, C., Brown, M., McCallum, B. and McAlister, S. (1995) *Intuition or Evidence?* (Buckingham: Open University Press).

Gipps, C. and Murphy, P. (1994) *A Fair Test? Assessment, Achievement and Equity* (Buckingham: Open University Press).

Good, T.L. and Grouws, D.A. (1975) 'Process-product relationships in 4th grade mathematics classrooms', Report for National Institute of Education (report number: NE-G-00-0-0123) (Columbia, MO: University of Missouri).

Gorard, S. (2001) 'An alternative account of Boys' Underachievement at school', *The Welsh Journal of Education* 10(2): 4–14.

Gorard, S., Rees, G. and Salisbury, J. (1999) 'Reappraising the apparent underachievement of boys at school', *Gender and Education* 11(4): 441–54.

Harlen, W. (ed.) (1994) *Enhancing Quality in Assessment* (London: Paul Chapman).

Harlen, W. and Deakin Crick, R. (2002) 'A systematic review of the impact of summative assessment and tests on students' motivation for learning' (EPPI-Centre review, version 1.1), in *Research Evidence in Education Library* (London: EPPI-Centre, Social Science research Unit, Institute of Education).

Harris, S., Nixon, J. and Ruddock, J. (1993) 'School work, homework and gender', *Gender and Education* 5(1): 3–15.

Herrnstein, R. J. and Murray, C. (1994) *The Bell Curve* (New York: Free Press).

James, M. (1998) *Using Assessment for School Improvement* (Oxford: Heinemann).

James, M. (2000) 'Measured lives: the rise of assessment as the engine of change in English schools', *The Curriculum Journal* 1(3): 343–64.

Jones, S. (1992) 'The assessment of mathematical modelling', unpublished MEd dissertation, University of Wales, Swansea.

Lloyd, J. G. (1999) *How Exams Really Work: Guide to GCSEs, AS and A levels* (London: Cassell).

Lowe, R. (1998) 'The educational impact of the eugenics movement', *International Journal of Educational Research* 27(8): 647–60.

Miliband, D. (2003) 'Excellence and opportunity from 14 to 19', a speech by David Miliband MP, Minister of State for school standards, 21 January 2003, Press notice 2003/0006, at *http://www.dfes.gov.uk/pns/* (accessed 1 June 2003).

Mortimore, P., Sammons, P. and Thomas, S. (1994) 'School effectiveness and value-added measures', *Assessment in Education* 1(3).

Bibliography

Murphy, R. (1997) 'Drawing outrageous conclusions from national assessment results: where will it all end?', *British Journal of Curriculum and Assessment* 7(2).

Nuttall, D. (1990) *Differences in Examination Performances*, RS1277/90 (London: London Research and Statistics Branch, ILEA).

OECD (2000) *Measuring Student Knowledge and Skills: The PISA 2000 Assessment of Reading, Mathematical and Scientific Literacy* (Paris: OECD).

Ofsted (1996) *Subjects and Standards. Issues for School Development Arising from Ofsted Inspection Findings 1994–5. Key Stages 3 and 4 and Post-16* (London: Her Majesty's Stationery Office).

Ofsted (1998) *Secondary Education 1993-1997: A Review of Secondary Schools in England* (London: The Stationery Office).

Ofsted (2003) *Annual Report of Her Majesty's Chief Inspector of Schools: Standards and Quality in Education 2001/02* (London: The Stationery Office).

OHMCI (1997) *Survey on the Relative Performance of Boys and Girls* (Cardiff: OHMCI).

Plucker, J. (1998) 'History of influences in the development of intelligence theory and testing', at *http://www.indiana.edu/~intell/map.html* (accessed 1 June 2003).

QCA (2001a) *Assessment for learning*, at *http://www.qca.org.uk/ca/5-14/afl/* (accessed June 2003).

QCA (2001b) *Using Assessment to Raise Achievement in Mathematics*, at *http: // www.qca.org.uk/ca/514/afl/afl_maths.pdf* (accessed 1 December 2001).

Ryan, J. and Williams, J. (2000) *Mathematical Discussions with Children 'Exploring Methods and Misconceptions as a Teaching Strategy'* (Manchester: University of Manchester Centre for Mathematics Education).

Sadler, D. R. (1989) 'Formative assessment and the design of instructional systems', *Instructional Science* 18: 119-44.

Sadler, D.R. (1998) 'Formative assessment: revisiting the territory', *Assessment in Education* 5(1): 77–84.

Salisbury, J., Rees, G. and Gorard, S. (1999) 'Accounting for the differential attainment of boys and girls at school', *School leadership and management* 19(4): 403–26.

Saunders, L. (1999a) 'A brief history of educational "value added": How did we get to where we are?' *School Effectiveness and School Improvement* 10(2): 233–56.

Saunders, L. (1999b) *'Value Added' Measurement of School Effectiveness: A Critical Review* (Slough: NFER).

Schagen, I. (1998) 'Adding value with value-added', paper in the proceedings of NFER's Annual Conference, at *http://www.nfer.ac.uk/conferences/value.htm*

SEAC (1991) *Teacher Assessment at Key Stage 3: An In-Service Resource, Mathematics* (London: HMSO).

Smithers, R. (2002) 'Overloaded exam system may lead to crisis matching rail chaos, heads warn', *Guardian*, Monday, 18 March 12002, at *http://www.guardian.co.uk* (accessed 1 June 2003).

Bibliography

Smithers, R. (2003) 'On your marks', *Guardian*, Tuesday, 29 April 2003, at *http://www.guardian. co.uk/* (accessed 1 June 2003).

Snow, R. E. (1996) 'Self-regulation as meta-conation', *Learning and Individual Difference* 8(3): 261–7.

Spearman, C. (1923) *Nature of 'Intelligence' and the Principles of Cognition* (London: Macmillan).

Stobart, G., Elwood, J. and Hayden, M. (1992a) *Differential Performance in Examinations at 16+: English and Mathematics* (London: SEAC).

Stobart, G., Elwood, J. and Quinlan, M. (1992b) 'Gender bias in examinations: How equal are the opportunities?' *British Educational Research Journal* 18(3): 261–76.

Sylva, K. (1994) 'School influences on children's development', *Journal of Child Psychology and Psychiatry* 35(1): 135–70.

Tanner, H. (1992) 'Teacher assessment of mathematics in the National Curriculum at Key Stage 3', *Welsh Journal of Education* 3(2): 27–34.

Tanner, H. (1997) 'Using and applying mathematics: developing mathematical thinking through practical problem-solving and modelling', unpublished PhD thesis, University of Wales, Swansea.

Tanner, H. and Jones, S. (1994) 'Using peer and self-assessment to develop modelling skills with students aged 11 to 16: A socio-constructive view', *Educational Studies in Mathematics* 27(4): 413–31.

Tanner, H. F. R. and Jones, S. A. (1995) 'Teaching mathematical thinking skills to accelerate cognitive development', paper in *The Proceedings of Psychol-*

ogy of Mathematics Education Conference (PME-19), Recife, Brazil, 3: 121–8.

Tanner, H. and Jones, S. (1999) 'Dynamic scaffolding and reflective discourse: the impact of teaching style on the development of mathematical thinking', in *The Proceedings of the 23rd Conference of the International Group for the Psychology of Mathematics Education (PME-23)*, Haifa 4: 257–64.

Tanner, H. and Jones, S. (2000a) 'Scaffolding for success: reflective discourse and the effective teaching of mathematical thinking skills', in T. Rowland and C. Morgan (eds), *Research in Mathematics Education Volume 2: Papers of the British Society for Research into Learning Mathematics*, (London: British Society for Research into Learning Mathematics, 19–32).

Tanner, H. and Jones, S. (2000b) *Becoming a Successful Teacher of Mathematics* (London: Routledge/Falmer).

Tanner, H. and Jones, S. (2003a) 'Assessing children's mathematical thinking in practical modelling situations', *Teaching Mathematics and its Applications* 21(4): 145–59.

Tanner, H. and Jones, S. (2003b) 'Self-efficacy in mathematics and students' use of self-regulated learning strategies during assessment events', paper in *The Proceedings of the 27th Conference of the International Group for the Psychology of Mathematics Education (PME27)*, Honolulu (in press).

Tanner, H., Jones, S. and Davies, A. (2002) *Developing Numeracy in the Secondary School* (London: David Fulton).

Bibliography

Thornton, K. (1999) 'Writing lessons for boys at age 11', *Times Educational Supplement*, 12 January 1999.

Tomlinson, M. (2002) Inquiry into 'A' level standards: final report (London: QCA).

Torrance, H. and Prior, J. (1998) *Investigating Formative Assessment: Teaching, Learning and Assessment in the Classroom* (Buckingham: Open University Press).

Von Glasersfeld, E. (ed.) (1991) *Radical Constructivism in Mathematics Education* (Dordrecht: Kluwer).

Weeden, P., Winter, J. and Broadfoot, P. (2002) *Assessment: What's in it for schools?* (London: Routledge/Falmer).

Wiliam, D. (1992) 'Some technical issues in assessment: A user's guide', *British Journal of Curriculum and Assessment* 2(3): 11–20.

Wiliam, D. (1996) 'Standards in examinations: A matter of trust?' *Curriculum Journal* 7(3) (Autumn): 293–306.

Wiliam, D. (1999a) 'Formative assessment in Mathematics: Part 1: Rich questioning' *Equals* 5(2) (Summer): 15–18.

Wiliam, D., (1999b) 'Formative assessment in Mathematics: Part 2: Feedback', *Equals* 5(3) (Autumn): 8–13.

Wiliam, D. (2000) 'Formative assessment in Mathematics: Part 3: The learner's role', *Equals* 6(1) (Summer): 18–22.

Wolters, C. A. and Rosenthal, H. (2000) 'The relation between students' motivational beliefs and their use of motivational regulation strategies', *International Journal of Educational Research* 33(7–8): 801–20.